Jane Austen

JANE AUSTEN
Tom Keymer

writing,

society,

politics

OXFORD
UNIVERSITY PRESS

OXFORD

UNIVERSITY PRESS

Great Clarendon Street, Oxford, OX2 6DP,
United Kingdom

Oxford University Press is a department of the University of Oxford.
It furthers the University's objective of excellence in research, scholarship,
and education by publishing worldwide. Oxford is a registered trade mark of
Oxford University Press in the UK and in certain other countries

First Edition published in 2020

Impression: 2

Published in the United States of America by Oxford University Press
198 Madison Avenue, New York, NY 10016, United States of America

British Library Cataloguing in Publication Data
Data available

Library of Congress Control Number: 2020932227

ISBN 978-0-19-886190-4

Printed in Great Britain by
Bell & Bain Ltd., Glasgow

for Pru

CONTENTS

ACKNOWLEDGEMENTS

Warm thanks to my publishers Andrea Keegan, Jenny Nugee, and Luciana O'Flaherty for their expert guidance throughout the preparation of this book, and to OUP's peer reviewers for the wise advice they contributed in the opening and closing stages. I did much of the writing during a visiting fellowship at All Souls College, Oxford, and I thank the Warden and Fellows for their generous hospitality. My thinking has been boosted over the years by fruitful conversations with many fine scholars of Jane Austen, among them Janine Barchas, Joe Bray, Linda Bree, Ed Copeland, Jenny Davidson, Jocelyn Harris, Freya Johnston, Heather King, Devoney Looser, Deidre Lynch, Juliet McMaster, Claude Rawson, Peter Sabor, Fiona Stafford, Kathryn Sutherland, Bharat Tandon, Karen Valihora, and Cindy Wall. I'm grateful to the keen undergraduates who have made it such a pleasure to teach the 'Austen and Her Contemporaries' course at the University of Toronto, to my outstanding teaching assistants Angela Du and Veronica Litt, and to the clever, sharp-eyed students who contributed research assistance and/or road-tested draft chapters: Dana Lew, Austin Long (who also created the index), Ryan Park, Sushani

Singh, Philip Trotter, and Rachael Tu. I thank Bodleian Library Publishing and Cambridge University Press for permission to include passages adapted from my contributions to K. Sutherland (ed.), *Jane Austen: Writer in the World* (2017), and J. Todd (ed.), *The Cambridge Companion to Pride and Prejudice* (2013).

LIST OF ILLUSTRATIONS

NOTE ON REFERENCES AND EDITIONS

Quotations from Jane Austen's writings are taken from the following editions, all of which (except Deirdre Le Faye's edition of the letters) appear in the Oxford World's Classics series. References to the novels are supplied parenthetically in the text by volume and chapter number; letters are cited by date. For other sources quoted below, see the 'References' section at the end of the volume.

Emma, ed. James Kinsley, introduction and notes by Adela Pinch (Oxford University Press, 2003)

Jane Austen's Letters, ed. Deirdre Le Faye, 4th edn (Oxford University Press, 2011)

Mansfield Park, ed. James Kinsley, introduction and notes by Jane Stabler (Oxford University Press, 2003)

Northanger Abbey, Lady Susan, The Watsons, Sanditon, ed. James Kinsley and John Davie, introduction and notes by Claudia L. Johnson (Oxford University Press, 2003)

Persuasion, ed. James Kinsley, introduction and notes by Deidre Shauna Lynch (Oxford University Press, 2004)

Pride and Prejudice, ed. James Kinsley, introduction and notes by Christina Lupton (Oxford University Press, 2019)

Sanditon, ed. Kathryn Sutherland (Oxford University Press, 2019)

Note on References and Editions

Sense and Sensibility, ed. John Mullan (Oxford University Press, 2019)

Teenage Writings, ed. Kathryn Sutherland and Freya Johnston (Oxford University Press, 2017)

Introduction

There are two big draws for visitors to Chawton, the Hampshire village where Jane Austen lived and wrote during the years when, if we count the immediately posthumous works, her six major novels were first published. By far the grander of the two is Chawton House, an Elizabethan manor where the unmarried, impecunious Austen was a welcome though fairly low-status guest: not quite hapless Miss Bates when she visits the Highbury elite in *Emma*, but in terms of social hierarchy it's not an irrelevant comparison. Chawton House was owned by Austen's brother Edward Knight, a wealthy man—wealthier than loaded, landed Mr Darcy in *Pride and Prejudice*—who had been adopted as an heir by rich cousins and mainly lived at Godmersham, Kent, on an even more desirable estate. The manor is now a charitable trust first established in the 1990s by Sandy Lerner, a serial entrepreneur—Cisco Systems, Urban Decay Cosmetics—and Austen devotee or 'Janeite' (a term popularized by Kipling's 1924 story about cultish novel-readers during the First World War). Media personalities and bestselling authors sometimes show up, and celebrity actors with Austen roles in their back catalogues.

Then there's the beautiful if far more modest house—'a very snug little cottage', as Mrs Dashwood puts it with resignation in *Sense and Sensibility* (I.vi)—that Austen shared as a home with three other women: her widowed mother, her beloved sister Cassandra, and their close friend Martha Lloyd. The women were settled in the cottage by Knight in 1809, and lived together in genteel obscurity, eking out a modest income and sharing the chores, until Austen moved to Winchester for medical reasons in 1817, the year of her death. It was here that she revised unpublished drafts from her youth (*Sense and Sensibility*, *Pride and Prejudice*, *Northanger Abbey*) and composed three further novels (*Mansfield Park*, *Emma*, *Persuasion*) more or less afresh. And it was here, completing Austen's slow transformation into a national icon, that Bank of England Governor Mark Carney unveiled the new design, based on a portrait sketch by Cassandra, that in 2017 replaced Charles Darwin on the £10 note (see Figure 1). The cottage, previously a roadside inn and later a lodging for labourers, is now the Jane Austen's House Museum. Visitors to its snug little rooms can see many evocative items: silhouette portraits; brooches and rings; a quilt stitched by Austen herself, an accomplished worker in textiles as well as texts.

Most evocative of all is a small walnut tripod table that Austen wrote on (see Figure 2). 'Some visitors hold their breath', says the museum website; 'others cry.' Austen's use of the table is well attested, though of course she wrote on countless others, in other locations, Bath or London as much as Chawton or before that the rectory of Steventon, her Hampshire birthplace and home until the age of 25.

Figure 1 Portrait sketch of Jane Austen by her sister Cassandra (*c.*1810), pencil and watercolour. The banknote version, copied from a stipple engraving of 1870, softens the tough-minded expression of the original sketch.

(The Steventon home can't be visited: Edward Knight demolished it in the 1820s to build something smarter for his son.) Austen wrote incessantly, even, we might say, obsessively. She's an instance of that Romantic-era phenomenon that the poet Samuel Taylor Coleridge called 'scribblomania'—the difference being that, unlike Coleridge, Austen could find no way of getting the scribble into print until the last few years of her life. *Sense and Sensibility*, *Pride and Prejudice*, and *Northanger Abbey* were all fully drafted before 1800, but didn't see publication until 1811, 1813, and 1817 respectively; *Mansfield Park* came out in 1814 and *Emma* in 1815; *Persuasion* was posthumously published in 1817 in a set with *Northanger Abbey*.

Figure 2 Early 18th-century tripod writing table belonging to Jane Austen, now at the Jane Austen's House Museum; a portable writing box used by her in the 1790s is in the British Library.

There's something uniquely eloquent about the walnut table. Perhaps its small size, a fitting match to the miniaturist perfection of Austen's art: 'the little bit (two Inches wide) of Ivory on which I work with so fine a Brush, as produces little effect after much labour', as she says in a late letter (17 December 1816). Materially, the table seems to embody the glimpses we get in family memoirs of Austen intently, creatively at work amidst bustling, sociable environments.

She had no separate study of her own—that *sine qua non*, for Virginia Woolf, of female authorship—and wrote 'in the general sitting-room, subject to all kinds of casual interruptions'. She used small sheets of paper that could be quickly tucked away when strangers called, or hidden under blotting paper, a nephew says. She'd sit by the fire with her needlework, a niece recalls, 'saying nothing for a good while, and then would suddenly burst out laughing, jump up and run across the room to a table where pens and paper were lying, write something down, and then come back to the fire and go on quietly working as before'. In Winchester, aged 41, she kept on writing 'whilst she could hold a pen, and with a pencil when a pen was become too laborious', her brother Henry reports. She was still writing just days before she died.

Then there are the manuscripts. The cult of the autograph was in its infancy when Austen's publishing career began, and the manuscripts of mere novels, a genre that had not yet achieved its Victorian prestige, were typically discarded or destroyed. Almost certainly, someone used the holograph manuscript of *Pride and Prejudice*, now among the world's most cherished novels, for waste paper or to light fires. Of the six completed novels, all we have in Austen's hand is a shortish section of *Persuasion*, which survives only because she rewrote and replaced it in the version sent to the printer. That said, we do have a good number of letters—161, though no doubt Austen wrote thousands—alongside shorter fictional works that were published long after her death. There are the teenage writings she produced at Steventon for family entertainment and then transcribed into notebook volumes that playfully, though also rather longingly, mimic print conventions. There are intermediate works such as her epistolary tale 'Lady Susan' (*c.*1794), her parodic 'Plan of a Novel' (*c.*1816), and her unfinished draft 'The Watsons' (1804), a story thought to have been abandoned because its themes of socioeconomic precarity and downward mobility were suddenly too close to the bone when her father, the Revd George Austen, died in 1805. Finally, there's the bold, energetic scrawl of 'Sanditon', the novel Austen began in the year of her death, heavily marked with deletions and substitutions that show just how strenuously she worked to achieve her signature effect of spontaneous lightness. In a much earlier letter to Cassandra, Austen apologizes for her 'sprawling' hand (22 January 1801), though stylistically her writing does anything but sprawl.

Is there also frustration to be detected in the 'Sanditon' hand, a sense of having broken into print too late, and of time now running out? Today, Austen is one of the most securely established literary classics in English, and alongside Shakespeare, perhaps the only pre-Victorian author who still finds a mass audience, globally as well as at home. It's easy to forget how hard she found it to break into print following the rejection of 'First Impressions' (the original version of *Pride and Prejudice*) in 1797, and then, in 1803, her sale of 'Susan' (which became *Northanger Abbey*) to a publisher who then simply shelved it. By the same token, it's easy to underestimate the adjustments, and no doubt the compromises, that Austen must have made in order to align her writing with the demands of a marketplace for fiction that was dominated by the commercial priorities of the circulating libraries, and by the tastes and desires of their fashionable subscribers. Austen would never have been published at all, and we would never have heard of her, had she not at least met the market halfway.

The results were astonishing, of course. In the most basic terms of fictional subgenre and literary structure, the six novels might in some ways have looked familiar enough: fluent, stylish exercises in domestic courtship fiction, elaborated over two or three volumes, tracking the efforts of their heroines to navigate society and the marriage market, and culminating in the happy ending—the 'perfect felicity' (*Northanger Abbey*, II.xvi)—of marriage to the eligible hero. All this was achieved, however, with unprecedented technical virtuosity, endlessly surprising comic verve, and subtle, penetrating insight into the psychology of individual characters and the dynamics of the social worlds they inhabit. Central to this virtuosity was Austen's mastery—though not, as was once assumed, her single-handed invention—of the breakthrough literary technique of free indirect style, which enabled her to narrate in a deft, economical third person while at the same time reflecting the inward experience and outward perspective of her protagonists.

In the face of artistic achievement of such great delicacy and power, it would be crass to assert that these were not quite the works Austen wanted to write—not the works she'd have written in other circumstances. The novel is nothing if not a market-driven genre, and since the time of Daniel Defoe, hard-nosed author of *Robinson Crusoe* (1719), great novelists have worked creatively with the grain of market forces to produce their masterpieces. In Austen's case, an important tradition of criticism takes her fiction very much at face value, as a body of work that articulates her authentic perspective on the world around her: a world thrown into turmoil by the social, political, and ideological shock of the French Revolution in 1789, and a world embroiled thereafter in global conflict (the Revolutionary and Napoleonic Wars) until almost the end of her life. In this view, we must read Austen as a fundamentally conservative writer whose fiction, while making satirical fun of corrupt or predatory individuals and even sometimes institutions, also broadly endorses the status quo, not least in endings that subsume her heroines' identities within those of their future husbands. In ways that bear comparison with the period's most powerful statement of conservative ideology, Edmund Burke's *Reflections on the Revolution in France* (1790), her novels locate moral value and communal harmony in the established traditions and time-honoured institutions of a hierarchical, patriarchal social order. Austen certainly documents the pressures, inequalities, and constraints of the world she describes, sympathizing deeply with the victims and laughing, sometimes scathingly, at the culprits. But at a time when literature often presented itself as a mode of social analysis, or as contributing to a political cause, her novels offer no recipe for overarching change, and make little effort to associate themselves with any particular project of reform.

It's hard to read much Austen, however, without sensing elements, and in particular satirical energies, that aren't fully explained by this kind of account. For other readers, a mutinous subtext lurks beneath the decorous, conformist surface of Austen's prose, and though working within the established conventions of courtship fiction, she was also a virtuoso of indirection who often signals dissent from the comfortable assumptions of her chosen genre. By focusing in most of her novels (*Emma* and *Persuasion* are the exceptions) on heroines who occupy positions of socioeconomic disadvantage in relation to those around them, and on the difficulties presented to them by the assumptions, conventions, and practices of their worlds, Austen converts courtship fiction to purposes more critical than those of mere fantasy or celebration. She was certainly not writing radical or proto-feminist fiction of the kind attempted by Mary Wollstonecraft, one of Burke's most strenuous interlocutors in the 1790s, whose novel *The Wrongs of Woman* (1798) was motivated by 'the desire of exhibiting the misery and oppression, peculiar to women, that arise out of the partial laws and customs of society'. But many of Austen's interests—in the trivializing bias of female education; in the costs to women of sensibility and other properly 'feminine' attributes or accomplishments; in patrilineal inheritance, property transmission, and instrumental marriage—align closely with those of Enlightenment feminism. Without Wollstonecraft's polemical directness, and in a mode always softened by the imperatives of comedy, Austen used her fiction to exhibit and explore, among much else, Wollstonecraftian questions about the society her protagonists inhabit. It's worth adding that, far from limiting the novels to their time and place, the effect has been to release them into ongoing, though unpredictable, kinds of relevance. One explanation for Austen's global popularity lies in her capacity to speak directly to readers navigating elaborate social conventions or rule-bound environments of different but analogous kinds in their own worlds.

Continuing debate along these lines has energized study of Austen since the 1970s, the defining early landmarks being Marilyn Butler's *Jane Austen and the War of Ideas* (1975) and Claudia L. Johnson's *Jane Austen: Women, Politics, and the Novel* (1988), the first of which argues for broadly speaking a conservative, Burkean Austen, the second for a progressive, and more nearly Wollstonecraftian, alternative. Yet perhaps the most striking feature of the novels as a whole, beyond any conservative attitude or radical animus they might here or there imply, is the facility and conviction with which they enter into multiple, sometimes competing, points of view. A novelist par excellence, Austen was imaginatively drawn to different perspectives, flexible and questioning, interested in representing experience from a range of positions. Her fiction assumes a world in which 'complete truth' belongs to no human disclosure (*Emma*, III.xi), and it encounters that world in a spirit of sceptical enquiry. Demonstrably, there were both conservative and progressive aspects to Austen's thinking, one or the other prevailing at different points in her writing, and sometimes simply coexisting in creative tension. In their varying ways, all the novels focus on the interpretative efforts of characters whose experience confronts them with uncertainties, contradictions, or mixed messages; the experience of reading the novels requires comparable efforts.

The following chapters approach Austen as a novelist in whom an implicitly Tory world view is frequently interrogated or disrupted by destabilizing ironies and irruptions of satirical anger that are no less real for the elegance and wit of their expression. My opening chapter explores the wayward, farcical impulse of Austen's teenage writings, which were never intended for publication and look experimentally forward to Victorian nonsense writing. Each of the remaining chapters is devoted to one of the six major novels, while at the same time addressing a key overarching theme in Austen criticism: politics and society (*Northanger Abbey*); Enlightenment feminism (*Sense and Sensibility*); narrative technique (*Pride and Prejudice*); national identity (*Emma*); slavery and empire (*Mansfield Park*); psychology and the passions (*Persuasion*). Historically, some of Austen's most insightful readers are to be found among the pioneering modernists of the 20th century, and their responses are sometimes used as points of entry into critical debate. Always to the fore is Woolf's conviction that Austen's art, for all its disarming air of tranquillity, even sometimes triviality, involves a constant challenge to pick up hints, pursue implications, and trace subcurrents wherever they lead. It's an art that insists we read between the lines, Woolf wrote of *Emma*: 'She stimulates us to supply what is not there.'

1

Jane Austen Practising

Jane Austen's cruelty is not the most obvious feature of much-loved novels like *Pride and Prejudice*, a work she once called 'too light & bright & sparkling;—it wants shade' (4 February 1813). For all their satirical brio, the novels exude sympathy and understanding, and that is much of their appeal. But Virginia Woolf was on to something important when she wrote about Austen's preference for mockery over pity, and her distaste for dewy-eyed forgiveness, when reviewing a selection of early manuscripts that caused a minor sensation when first published in 1922. 'Never, even at the emotional age of fifteen, did she round upon herself in shame, obliterate a sarcasm in a spasm of compassion, or blur an outline in a mist of rhapsody', Woolf wrote. The newly available juvenilia helped readers tune into an aspect of Austen's art that was always there, and by 1940 the critic and psychologist D. W. Harding could write about her, in a landmark essay, as the great exponent of what he called 'regulated hatred'. In her earliest writing, the imaginative cruelty is in fact deliciously unregulated, and coexists with other features that challenge received opinions about Austen—opinions the Victorian custodians of her reputation, who suppressed nearly all of it, were determined to uphold. Not only are the norms of compassion suspended in these youthful skits, but also many related norms: of decorum, morality, language, and narrative logic. Austen's manuscript works are striking achievements in their own right, and point to aspects of the published novels we might otherwise miss.

The family milieu

Born in 1775, soon after the American War of Independence broke out, Austen grew up in comfortable respectability, if not quite prosperity, among the large family of the Revd George Austen, a clergyman who held two modest livings in Hampshire and took boarding pupils on the side. Notable among her seven siblings are Cassandra, Austen's elder (and only) sister, and Frank and Charles, the closest to her in age (Charles was her only junior in the family), who both became naval officers during the French Revolutionary War and rose to the rank of admiral. Another brother, Henry, was by turns militia officer, banker, bankrupt, and finally cleric. More helpful for the long-term security of the family, especially Jane and Cassandra (neither married), was Edward, an older brother whose adoption as heir to a wealthy cousin eventually brought him an income of £15,000 a year: half as much again as Mr Darcy. When the money kicked in, however, it's fair to say that Edward gave no more than he had to.

It was in this busy, happy environment that the teenage writings were composed, between 1787 and 1793, as handwritten documents for family circulation and scripts for comic recital (Austen was a virtuoso performer of her own prose, which Henry said was 'never heard to so much advantage as from her own mouth'). She then transcribed the twenty-seven surviving items into archly labelled mock books that mimicked print conventions, as though to form a wildly precocious *Collected Works*: 'Volume the First', 'Volume the Second', 'Volume the Third'. Even after her career as a published author at last took off in 1811, the volumes remained in use by the family as agents of domestic sociability. Austen's nephew and niece, James Edward (Austen-Leigh) and Anna (Lefroy), contributed their own brief continuations of one item, the micro-novel 'Evelyn'; James Edward revised another, 'Kitty, or the Bower' (and it was probably he who changed the title to the more formal 'Catharine'). The only item to see print over the next century was one of the least interesting, 'The Mystery, an unfinished Comedy', which in 1871 was included by James Edward— now a bewhiskered, fox-hunting septuagenarian—in his *Memoir of Jane Austen*, the book that enshrined her Victorian reputation. He included this fragment, however, with embarrassment. Like the rest of his revered aunt's 'juvenile effusions', it was flimsy and puerile, but worth recording 'as a specimen of the kind of transitory amusement which Jane was continually supplying to the family party'.

Effusion, transitory amusement: the words are worth dwelling on. The first of them carried a certain prestige in Austen's day, when Coleridge and Wordsworth, among others, employed it to distinguish particular poems as spontaneous, authentic outflows of creative imagination. High praise was also intended in *Northanger Abbey*, where Austen hails novels by Frances Burney and Maria Edgeworth, her leading female precursors, as 'the liveliest effusions of wit and humour...in the best chosen language' (I.v). In Victorian usage, however, *effusion* took on a pejorative edge, implying the absence of disciplining intelligence or structuring art. That criticism remained in play when the influential Austen editor R. W. Chapman, even as he ushered more juvenilia into print in 1933, worried about publishing 'such effusions as these...and it may be that we have enough already of Jane Austen's early scraps'. Chapman's comment may explain why the last of the scraps (the surreal 'Evelyn' and the mischievous 'Kitty') did not reach print until 1951.

Transitory speaks for itself: fleeting, fugitive, disposable— though these volumes are now among the most cherished literary manuscripts in England, the more so because just one fragment (a pair of draft *Persuasion* chapters) survives from the major novels. But what about *amusement*? Here is another word with a double edge, meaning not only to entertain but also, at least potentially, to distract or mislead, like the 'unsafe amusements' of amateur theatricals in *Mansfield Park* (II.ii). In the *Memoir*, Austen-Leigh quotes an anecdote from his sister Caroline—another fun-loving Regency child turned crusty Victorian—in which Aunt Jane warns her against writing too much while too young, and confesses of her own output 'that she knew writing stories was a great amusement, and *she* thought a harmless one, though many people, she was aware, thought otherwise'.

Nonsense and insensibility

This anxiety among Austen's heirs about the potential of the juvenilia to undermine her standing as a serious novelist—a proto-Victorian moralist and domestic realist—did not preclude real alertness to the qualities that might do the damage. For Caroline, the teenage writings didn't so much anticipate the novels as contradict their ethos and effect: it was 'remarkable that the early workings of her mind should have been in burlesque, and comic exaggeration, setting at nought all rules of probable or possible—when of all her finished and later writings, the exact contrary is the characteristic'. Caroline summed up Austen's juvenilia as 'clever nonsense', and her brother concurred. These early stories were 'generally intended to be nonsensical', though at least 'the nonsense has much spirit in it'.

Nonsense is of course a disparaging term: literally a negation of sense, that core value of the published novels, or so *Sense and Sensibility* would suggest. Yet even as the word suggested itself to Austen's heirs, nonsense was also emerging, and gaining prestige, as a fresh, startlingly disruptive literary mode. Consciously or otherwise, they seemed to conceive the juvenilia as heralding not the towering achievements of George Eliot or other classic novelists but instead the playful capering of Lewis Carroll, who pushed his games with language, logic, and representation in *Alice's Adventures in Wonderland* (1865) to fresh extremes in his madcap nonsense-poem *The Hunting of the Snark* (1876). The nonsense label was used with greatest emphasis by Edward Lear, whose zanily inventive *A Book of Nonsense*

(1846) was followed, just as 'The Mystery' appeared in Austen-Leigh's *Memoir*, by the verbal pyrotechnics of *Nonsense Songs, Stories, Botany and Alphabets* (1871), containing 'The Owl and the Pussycat' and other deadpan fragments of topsy-turvydom.

Modern accounts of nonsense literature find it not only playful but also subversive. They emphasize the dizzying contradictions and ruptures that nonsense writing leaves unexplained, and the function of linguistic havoc, irrational logic, and representational muddle in placing standard ways of seeing, thinking, and judging at an ironic distance. With its delight in suspending moral norms and violating narrative expectations, the genre becomes a wayward antidote to the realist novel in its Victorian heyday, wittily defamiliarizing everyday language, value systems, and ways of knowing.

If Austen's teenage writings were nonsense by these criteria, not just youthful frivolities but texts at odds with the published novels' allegiance to morality and truth, it becomes easy to see why they had to be kept under wraps. Yet we can also see why, when the juvenilia finally reached print in the modernist era, they seemed so refreshing. In his introduction to *Love & Freindship and Other Early Works* (the title used in 1922 for 'Volume the Second'), G. K. Chesterton proposed a radical realignment of Austen's place in literary tradition, likening the contents to 'the great burlesques of Peacock or Max Beerbohm', or to the carnivalesque satire of Rabelais and Dickens. This was the edition Woolf was reviewing when, throwing off the suffocating blanket of Austenolatry (a term coined by her father Leslie Stephen), she celebrated instead the 'sheer nonsense' of 'Volume the Second', and its clear-eyed refusal to be decorous or deferential in the interests of conformity or good taste. Woolf concluded that to read the teenage writings was 'to listen . . . to Jane Austen practising'. But if so, Austen was practising for something beyond the role of polite novelist.

Unbecoming Jane

In our own day, feminist criticism has emphasized the transgressive quality of these early works. In one influential line of argument, if the teenage writings are rehearsals for anything at all, they're rehearsals for a road not taken. Central to this view are the long years of frustration and blockage endured by Austen before breaking into print in her midthirties: a process requiring capitulation to, or at least compromise with, the limiting norms of published fiction at the time. For the feminist critic Margaret Anne Doody, the conformist genre of courtship fiction to which Austen had to adapt 'was not the appropriate home of social criticism or free aesthetic play—still less of moral questioning'. In this context, for Doody, the special value of the teenage manuscripts lies in the trace they leave of disruptive instincts that Austen had to suppress in order to get published at all. 'Her early writing is rough, violent, sexy, joky'; it tells us 'what Austen might have sounded like without such domestication'. In other words, the Austen we listen to here is not the author she would become; it's the one she wouldn't.

More harmonious accounts exist of the relationship between the juvenilia and the novels. For Juliet McMaster, author of the most detailed study of the juvenilia, the achievements of the mature fiction—'all that restraint in the service of exactness and the *mot juste*, all the fine moral imagination that can trace the delicate intricacies of an evolving relationship'—look all the greater for their origins in uninhibited youthful gusto. Even in accounts like these, however, the emphasis falls on contrast, and it has become second nature for Austen critics in general to characterize the two bodies of work in binary terms: on one hand, the insouciant, violent, outrageous early manuscripts; on the other, the poised, nuanced, decorous published novels. McMaster's account of the contrast turns on parody, and she demonstrates how the juvenilia send up the conventions and clichés of the routine sentimental novels that filled the fashionable circulating libraries of the day. There are traceable connections to kinds of fiction that Austen and her siblings—'great Novel-readers & not ashamed of being so' (18 December 1798)—must have binge-read in the Steventon rectory. 'Love and Freindship' is a cruelly accelerated burlesque of Eliza Nugent Bromley's *Laura and Augustus* (1784), a 500-page tear-jerker that one weary book reviewer described as 'frequently interesting'.

More broadly, the teenage writings target the tired formulae and creaking conventions of the genre as a whole, though with relish alongside the ridicule. In *Northanger Abbey*, Austen would distance herself from the lofty put-downs that circulating-library novels tended to elicit—'Let us leave it to the Reviewers . . . to talk in threadbare strains of the trash with which the press now groans' (I.v)—and there's no patronizing rhetoric in these early skits. It's entirely in a spirit of fun that Austen sends up the unctuous dedications and flatulent prefaces that routinely introduced novels, and each of the twenty-seven items is playfully dedicated to a relative or friend. 'The beautifull Cassandra, a novel in twelve Chapters' is offered to Austen's sister in compliment to her 'Virtues innumerable' (the longest chapter has forty-nine words, and Cassandra does nothing much except bilk tradesmen). One poker-faced dedication presents solemn moral lessons to her niece Anna, who 'will derive from them very important Instructions, with regard to your Conduct'; Anna was seven weeks old.

Other standard fictional devices come in for satirical exaggeration: the gratuitous interpolated tales often used to pad out novels ('Will you favour us with your Life & adventures?', a young lady is asked as she writhes with a broken leg in a gamekeeper's trap; she cheerfully obliges); the evocation of debilitating sensibility ('It was too pathetic for the feelings of Sophia and myself—We fainted Alternately on a Sofa'); the crippling artificiality of epistolary novels: 'Dear Maud | Beleive me I'm happy to hear of your Brother's arrival. I have a thousand things to tell you, but my paper will only permit me to add that I am y^r affec.^{t} Freind | Amelia Webster.'

Many of these generic clichés were still limping on in 1816, the likely date of Austen's tongue-in-cheek 'Plan of a Novel', which trains its fire on the recycled plot-devices and rhetorical platitudes of didactic fiction, and on its occasional maladroit gestures of social criticism. Eventually, 'the poor Father...after 4 or 5 hours of tender advice & parental Admonition to his miserable Child, expires in a fine burst of Literary Enthusiasm, intermingled with Invectives against Holders of Tythes'. In this context, we can see the teenage writings as giving notice, parodically, of a vein of self-reflexive satire that remained alive throughout Austen's maturity. They mock tastes and expectations that Austen had to accommodate in the published novels, though she made the adjustment with supreme creative intelligence and ongoing flourishes of fun. These include her joke about the inevitability of a marriage ending in *Northanger Abbey*, as betrayed by the book's material form: 'my readers . . . will see in the tell-tale compression of the pages before them, that we are all hastening together to perfect felicity' (II.xvi).

The worst-chosen language

Yet we must probe beyond the fairly stable categories of parody and burlesque to get the full measure of Austen's nonsense in these precocious texts. The play of wit in the juvenilia runs far in excess of satirical function, and an obvious example lies in Austen's exuberant wordplay. There are the outlandish names of her fictional locations: Crankhumdunberry ('Frederic & Elfrida'), Pammydiddle ('Jack & Alice'), or the charmed environment where the hero of 'Sir William Mountague' falls simultaneously in love 'with the 3 Miss Cliftons of Kilhoobery Park'. There are her risqué character names: in 'Frederic & Elfrida' alone, the inspired 'Jezalinda' (part sentimental heroine, part biblical whore) and 'Captain Roger of Buckinghamshire' (the double entendre of *rogering* was a staple of satire at the time). Overall, there's too much sexual innuendo to explain away as chance, and some of it points in unexpected directions. As in *Mansfield Park*, with Mary Crawford's pointed gag about admirals, rears, and vices in the navy—'Now, do not be suspecting me of a pun, I entreat' (I.vi)—sodomy comes into view in 'The History of England', written 'By a partial, prejudiced, & ignorant Historian'. A send-up of derivative textbooks like Oliver Goldsmith's four-volume *History of England* of 1771 (Austen's copy survives, with her marginal notes), Austen's version zanily casts the upstart page-boy Lambert Simnel as 'Widow of Richard [III]'. She goes on to praise the famously bisexual James I for the 'keener penetration' he shows with his male favourites.

Beyond these deft touches of obscene periphrasis, it may have been Austen's exuberant list-making that reminded Chesterton of Rabelais, with the delight she takes in each rush of incongruous nouns. Witness the fleet of trophy carriages in 'Memoirs of Mr Clifford': 'a Coach, a Chariot, a Chaise, a Landeau, a Landeaulet, a Phaeton, a Gig, a Whisky, an italian Chair, a Buggy, a Curricle & a wheel barrow.' Or the meat feast tackled by Charlotte in 'Frederic & Elfrida'— 'a young Leveret, a brace of Partridges, a leash of Pheasants & a Dozen of Pigeons'—soon after inadvertently accepting two different marriage proposals. Charlotte drowns herself a paragraph later, to be commemorated in a gloriously clunky epitaph to one who 'Threw her sweet Body & her lovely face | Into the Stream that runs thro' Portland Place'. Elsewhere Austen highlights her enjoyment of ill-placed banality by improvising bogus proverbial phrases: 'Tho' . . . Frederic was as bold as brass yet in other respects his heart was as soft as cotton.' She revels in jarring mismatches between polite and demotic language: 'I shall trouble Mr Stanly for a Little of the fried Cow heel & Onion', says a genteel lady in 'The Visit'. Then there are the gratuitous intrusions of epic diction. The hero of 'Jack & Alice' (named Charles—Jack eventually appears, but dies of drink a sentence later) is 'of so dazzling a Beauty that none but Eagles could look him in the Face'. Throughout the volumes, to recall Austen's compliment to Burney and Edgeworth in *Northanger Abbey*, it's as though she's seeking out the worst-chosen language.

Similar incongruities are at work at the level of representation, typically without explanation. The plot of 'Evelyn', in which a tourist casually asks to be given his hosts' perfect landed estate and immediately gets it, operates according to a logic that is never disclosed (the hosts throw in their daughter, with apologies for the subpar dowry of £10,000). In gleeful violation of formal realism, even rudimentary standards of literary competence, we find absurd hyperbole—'Emma . . . continued in tears the remainder of her Life' ('Henry & Eliza'); litotes—'Our neighbourhood was small, for it consisted only of your Mother' ('Love and Freindship'); contradiction—'his name was Lindsay . . . I shall conceal it' ('Love and Freindship'); tautology—'Tho' Benevolent & Candid, she was Generous & sincere' ('Jack & Alice'); bathos—'A Grove of full-grown Elms sheltered us from the East—. A Bed of full-grown Nettles from the West—' ('Love and Freindship'); sheer gratuitous absurdity—'he regularly sent home a large Newfoundland Dog every Month to his family' ('Detached peices'). The sexed-up lovers of 'Frederic & Elfrida' are unable to marry 'on account of the tender years of the young couple, Rebecca being but

36 & Captain Roger little more than 63'; a few pages later the obstacle disappears, 'seven days being now expired'.

A favourite device is one that Laurence Sterne (a satirist Austen echoes in the elms/nettles passage quoted above) called 'the Cervantic humour . . . of describing silly and trifling events with the circumstantial pomp of great ones'. Elaborate narrative attention is forever being lavished on the wrong thing. A suspenseful elopement tale is interrupted by a long conversation about red-cheeked complexions; paragraphs are devoted to a family debate about opening, or not opening, a door. Without registering the least surprise, 'Henry & Eliza' merges wildly incompatible narrative settings, presided over by 'the Dutchess of F.', who fluctuates between alternative roles as enlightened modern aristocrat and brutal medieval warlord. In the first, she attends assemblies and arranges advantageous matches; in the second, she builds dungeons and plans tortures for her enemies, and 'sent out after them 300 armed Men, with orders not to return without their Bodies, dead or alive'.

This may have been a joke about the uneven historical novels of the late 18th century, still incongruously couched in the language of modern sensibility, before the genre hit its stride with Walter Scott a generation later. It's a joke resumed in the playful anachronisms of the medallion portraits contributed by Cassandra to 'The History of England', which represent Henry IV as a rouged, peruked fop in frock-coat and ruffles, and Henry V as a strutting officer with tricorn hat and gold epaulettes: possibly a gentle caricature of Henry Austen, who was soon to become a militia officer (see Figure 3). 'This Monarch was famous only for his not live for ever, but falling ill, his son the Prince of Wales came and took away the crown; whereupon the King made a long speech, for which I must refer the Reader to Shakespear's Plays, & the Prince made a still longer. Things being thus settled between them the King died, & was succeeded by his son Henry who had previously beat Sir William Gascoigne.

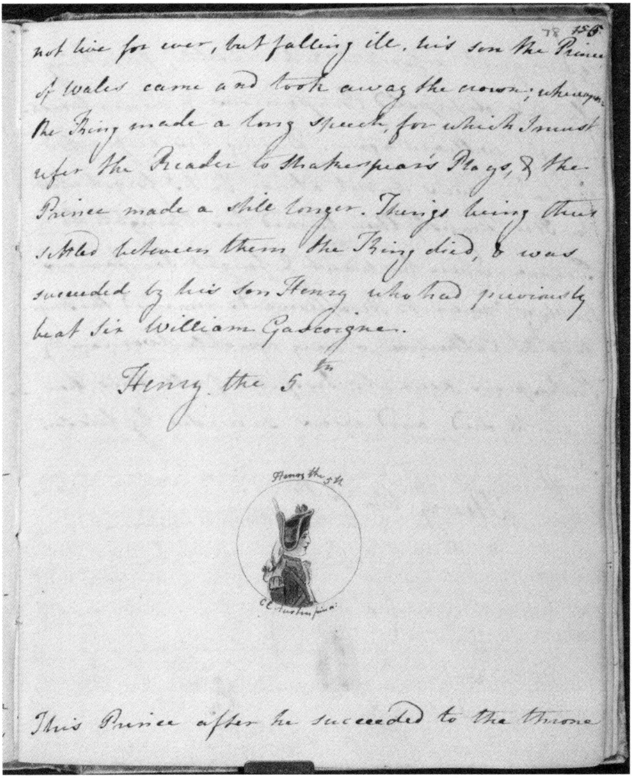

Henry the 5th

This Prince after he succeeded to the throne

Figure 3 A page from Austen's manuscript 'History of England' (1791), written in the voice of 'a partial, prejudiced, & ignorant Historian'; the ironic roundel illustration is by her sister Cassandra.

Beauty', writes Austen of Edward IV; the portrait shows a slouching 18th-century artisan, slovenly and porcine.

Cudgels and traps

Highlighting these effects of absurdity is Austen's staunch refusal to recognize that anything is awry. Her characteristic narrative stance is one of deadpan neutrality, of unsurprised, even uninterested, acceptance of cruelty and violence, of cheerful, moral insouciance and emotional anaesthesia, in a vein that looks forward to Evelyn Waugh. It's a matter of mere report, not comment, when a visitor to Crankhumdunberry grotesquely mangles the 18th-century 'beauties of the mind' trope:

> Lovely & too charming Fair one, notwithstanding your forbidding Squint, your greasy tresses & your swelling Back, which are more frightfull than imagination can paint or pen describe, I cannot refrain from expressing my raptures, at the engaging Qualities of your Mind, which so amply atone for the Horror, with which your first appearance must ever inspire the unwary visitor.

The addressee (Rebecca, target of Roger from Buckingham's lust) takes no offence, and no other character sees anything amiss. The same is true when, with a perfectly timed switch from abstract Latinate generalities to material Anglo-Saxon particulars, Austen explodes the pastoral idyll of 'Henry & Eliza', which opens with 'Sir George and Lady Harcourt . . . superintending the Labours of their Haymakers, rewarding the industry of some by smiles of approbation, & punishing the idleness of others, by a cudgel' (Box 1).

BOX 1   *Opening of 'Henry & Eliza'*

As Sir George and Lady Harcourt were superintending the Labours of their Haymakers, rewarding the industry of some by smiles of approbation, & punishing the idleness of others, by a cudgel, they perceived lying closely concealed beneath the thick foliage of a Haycock, a beautifull little Girl not more than 3 months old.

Touched with the enchanting Graces of her face & delighted with the infantine tho' sprightly answers she returned to their many questions, they resolved to take her home &, having no Children of their own, to educate her with care & cost.

Being good People themselves, their first & principal care was to incite in her a Love of Virtue & a Hatred of Vice, in which they so well succeeded (Eliza having a natural turn that way herself) that when she grew up, she was the delight of all who knew her.

Beloved by Lady Harcourt, adored by Sir George & admired by all the world, she lived in a continued course of uninterrupted Happiness, till she had attained her eighteenth year, when happening one day to be detected in stealing a banknote of 50£, she was turned out of doors by her inhuman Benefactors.

'Cudgel' is a beautiful ambush on Austen's part, its approach hidden by elegant parallelism ('rewarding the industry … punishing the idleness') and the vapid clichés of paternalism ('superintending', 'smiles of approbation'). But Austen makes no more of the joke than this, and instead moves briskly on to further irruptions of narrative mayhem: the sprightly conversation of a three-month-old baby; the unexplained portrayal of the Harcourts as both virtuous and inhuman; the unruffled report of Eliza's thieving alongside praise for her exalted mind. This is a world of random, abrupt violence, in which lovers are casually shot by their rivals and jealous ladies murder their friends, but no one seems to mind, or even much notice. The narrator is always interested in something else, whether the happy consequences for her marriage plot—'Sir William shot Mr Stanhope; the lady had then no reason to refuse him' ('Sir William Mountague')—or the proper language of commemoration. When one heroine dies—'Sukey . . . jealous of her superior charms took her by poison from an admiring World' ('Jack & Alice')—we might almost miss the operative word 'poison' amidst the surrounding fluff (superior charms, admiring world).

Other characters enjoy cartoon-like immunity from harm, and this too offers no grounds for remark. When a romantically roaming lover has her leg broken 'in one of the steel traps so common in gentlemen's grounds', she's instantly healed by a passer-by with no surgical experience—a circumstance the narrator notes but does not explain. In a beautifully managed example of comic syllepsis (where a verb does double service for ill-matched nouns), poachers' traps are recognized as improper in courtship: 'Oh! cruel Charles to wound the hearts & legs of all the fair' ('Jack & Alice'). But Charles's rough wooing is soon forgotten in the riot of drunkenness, adultery, murder, and hanging that then ensues, none of it with much sign of authorial disapproval. Sometimes—a trick Austen learned from Henry Fielding—criminal conduct is slyly endorsed by a rogue adverb or a tactical switch from moral to aesthetic criteria. In 'Love and Freindship', the hero and heroine enjoy 'a considerable sum of Money which Augustus had gracefully purloined from his Unworthy father's Escritoire'. 'The History of England' applauds Henry VIII for despoiling monasteries and leaving them in ruins, an act 'of infinite use to the landscape of England'.

For the modern novelist Anthony Burgess, 'the British nonsense tradition, like the surrealist one that succeeded it, is only a bizarre way of making sense'. The nonsense of Austen's manuscript mock-books is bizarre indeed in the sense it makes. Yet the distinguishing features of this nonsense—stylistic exuberance; radical incongruity; unexplained or unresolved paradox; suspended norms of perception and judgement; arbitrary subversions of narrative logic; unperturbed acceptance of narrated chaos—are aspects of Austen's repertoire worth keeping in mind. She would never write for print in the same spirit of unconstrained ridicule or comic violence, just as the pitiless wit of her private letters was not for publication ('I suppose she happened unawares to look at her husband', Austen notoriously writes (27 October 1798) when an acquaintance miscarries). Rather than disappear, however, these aspects of Austen's satirical genius still lurk beneath the surface of her novels, occasionally breaking that surface in startling ways.

2

The Terrors of
Northanger Abbey

Austen's popularity is often strongest in times of crisis, when the serene world of the novels can seem to offer therapeutic escape. During the First World War, Herbert Brett-Smith, an Oxford scholar tasked to choose suitable reading for wounded soldiers, prescribed Austen for patients with severe shellshock. In 1943, at the height of the Second World War, Winston Churchill had *Pride and Prejudice* read to him while critically ill with pneumonia, and sensed in the novel a consoling immunity to the geopolitical upheavals of its time. 'What calm lives they had, those people!' Churchill later reflected: 'No worries about the French Revolution, or the crashing struggle of the Napoleonic Wars. Only manners controlling natural passion so far as they could.' His comment perfectly catches the private struggles of Austen's characters, but finds no trace of public struggles. This was the prevailing view, and a generation later a study entitled *Jane Austen and the French Revolution* (1979), by the historian Warren Roberts, aroused widespread incredulity. There were French windows in the novels, French cooks, and

French bread, but there was no French Revolution. The nearest Austen came to it was a mention in *Northanger Abbey* of the novelist Frances Burney's émigré husband (General Alexandre d'Arblay, a liberal who fled to England in 1792), though in the later novels occasional French warships—privateers, frigates—indicate the Napoleonic context.

Yet is this view of Austen as a novelist somehow out of her time—or a novelist, at least, whose documentation of private life neglects the shaping influence of public context—a view we have to accept? Not necessarily. Biographers often note immediately personal ways in which the long-term upheaval precipitated by the French Revolution impinged on Austen's mind. There was the influence of her glamorous cousin (and future sister-in-law) Eliza, whose royalist husband, Jean-François de Feuillide, was guillotined in Paris in 1794. There were the harrowing, though professionally rewarding, experiences of the brothers closest to her in age, Frank and Charles, who both saw wide-ranging naval service throughout the Revolutionary and Napoleonic Wars. More important is the impact on the novels, albeit an impact marked at every point by Austen's habits of indirection. In *Northanger Abbey*, she deftly registers the fraught atmosphere of the revolution decade as it haunts her characters' imaginations: the sense of living in a society surrounded, as Henry Tilney puts it, by 'voluntary spies' (II.ix), or on the alert, like his sister Eleanor, for newspaper reports of city streets 'flowing with blood' (I.xiv). More emphatically, Austen registers this atmosphere by playing with witty virtuosity on the literature of terror, and specifically the Gothic novel, as it pervaded the marketplace for print in the 1790s.

Literature and politics in the 1790s

In the upper ranks of society, the foremost anxiety was that revolutionary upheaval would leap the Channel. Unrest of the kind feared by Eleanor Tilney did occasionally erupt, and in 1792, shortly before staying with the Austens at Steventon, Eliza de Feuillide was caught in a riot in Mount Street, London. Writing to another cousin, Phylly Walter, she describes with alarm 'the noise of the populace, the drawn swords & pointed bayonets of the guards, the fragments of brick & mortar thrown on every side, one of which had nearly killed my Coachman, the firing at one end of the street'. Meanwhile, new political associations were demanding radical reforms including universal male suffrage and annual parliaments. Their activities were closely monitored by government as well as self-appointed spies, and led in 1794 to treason indictments involving, among others, the novelist Thomas Holcroft. Even Wordsworth and Coleridge, in a bizarre episode of Home Office paranoia, were spied on in 1797 after being reported by a suspicious neighbour.

For revolution sympathizers, the reign of terror under Robespierre and the Jacobins in France was paralleled in England by the alarmist ministry of William Pitt. Given the massive scale of bloodletting across the Channel, this comparison was absurdly exaggerated, but it was also widely voiced. For a Norwich radical of 1794, Pitt was introducing 'a system of TERROR . . . infinitely more pernicious in its tendency than France ever knew'.

These events also transformed the literary world. In his prescient *Reflections on the Revolution in France* (1790), a work often held to epitomize the conservative attitudes of Austen's milieu, the Whig statesman Edmund Burke warned of the practical dangers of revolutionary idealism. His book asserted the stabilizing values of social hierarchy, inherited rights, and gradualist reform within a constitutional tradition, and fired up the opposition press. Tom Paine's incendiary—and alarmingly cheap and accessible—*Rights of Man* (1791) was the most conspicuous counterblast; another was Mary Wollstonecraft's *Vindication of the Rights of Men* (1790), followed two years later by the ground-breaking *Vindication of the Rights of Woman*, which extended Wollstonecraft's arguments into gender politics.

Years later, in *Emma*, Austen plays ironically on the key terms of the revolution debate, when a proposal to skip supper becomes 'an infamous fraud upon the rights of men and women' (II.xi). But at the time the debate spilled very directly into the pages of novels, not least because radical political theorists were often keen to promote their ideas through fiction. In her trenchant posthumous novel *The Wrongs of Woman* (1798), Wollstonecraft's heroine likens wedlock to the tyrannies of *ancien-régime* France: 'Marriage had bastilled me for life.' The best-known 'English Jacobin' novel of the period is William Godwin's powerful *Things as They Are; or, The Adventures of Caleb Williams* (1794), about the trickle-down effects in private life of political despotism. With its focus on surveillance, pursuit, and incarceration, the novel suggests a pervasive context of government repression. Godwin later claimed to have been pressed to discard his politically charged preface in an environment where 'Terror was the order of the day' and 'even the humble novelist might be shown to be con-structively a traitor'.

Of course, not all novelists were Jacobin fellow-travellers. In response to polemical works like *Caleb Williams* or Holcroft's *Anna St Ives* (1792), conservative authors extolled the virtues of loyalty, subordination, and domestic and social duty within the framework of an existing, though by no means always perfect, hierarchical order. In the Cheap Repository Tracts produced by Hannah More and other evangelicals in the mid-1790s, fiction became a vehicle for religious didacticism. The decade's most conspicuous trend was the fashion for Gothic fiction, which reached its zenith with Ann Radcliffe's bestselling romance *The Mysteries of Udolpho* (1794) and Matthew Lewis's *The Monk* (1796). A literature of terror that included in its gory repertoire out-landish stories of abduction and atrocity, spine-tingling occult or supernatural effects, and a fervid rhetoric of sublime description, Gothic was a varied mode. But certain basic features were widely shared, and became, in particular, the stock in trade of the Minerva Press, a specialist publisher of Gothic and other fiction. These novels were typified by tem-porally or geographically remote settings—often medieval, often Mediterranean—in which enlightened modern con-straints on plot and action—manners and morals, customs and laws—were in abeyance. By locating climactic plot events in the winding labyrinths and gloomy recesses of ancient monasteries or ruined castles, they cultivated an atmosphere laden with enthralling psychosexual connotation.

By the end of the decade, it was commonplace for maga-zine critiques with titles like 'Terrorist Novel Writing' (1798) to ridicule the Gothic for its tendency 'to make *terror* the *order of the day*, by confining the heroes and heroines in old gloomy castles, full of spectres, apparitions, ghosts, and dead men's bones'. Yet the bloody horrors and eerie phantasmagoria of these works were not just sensationalist routines. With their daggers and prisons, their bloodshed and phantoms, the best Gothic novels also speak—not as conscious metaphor, but in subliminal ways—to the public atmosphere of turmoil, anxiety, and shock in which they were written and read. For the Marquis de Sade, in a remarkable essay of 1799, the imaginative world of Radcliffe and Lewis 'was the necessary offspring of the revolutionary upheaval which affected the whole of Europe'. With her usual deft touch, Austen makes the same connection when, in *Northanger Abbey*, her heroine Catherine Morland is thrilled that 'something very shocking indeed, will soon come out in London'—meaning a new novel filled with murders and horrors. Austen runs with the resulting confusion for a page or more, as Eleanor frets about conspiracies, riots, and the government's failure to prevent them. It falls to Henry to clear up the misunderstanding when he teases Eleanor for picturing 'a mob of three thousand men assembling in St. George's Fields, the Bank attacked, the Tower threatened, the streets of London flowing with blood' (I.xiv), when nothing more was meant than a sensationalist novel. The analogy between Gothic horror and sociopolitical turmoil is too emphatic to be quite dispelled, however. For the remainder of *Northanger Abbey*, the imaginary terrors of fiction intertwine in unexpected ways with the real dangers of life in the everyday world.

Novels in manuscript and print

Ensconced in the rectory at Steventon, Austen was comfortably removed from public turbulence when she began drafting full-length novels in the mid-1790s, and she was not to publish the first of them until much later. But this was one of the two most fertile periods in her creative life, a point recognized, albeit sometimes too bluntly, by critics who divide her output into two key phases: the 'Steventon years' in which *Northanger Abbey*, *Sense and Sensibility*, and *Pride and Prejudice* were drafted, and the 'Chawton years' when *Mansfield Park*, *Emma*, and *Persuasion* were composed (and all six novels underwent final revision). The chronology will never be entirely certain, but it seems clear from family memoranda that *Sense and Sensibility*, the first Austen novel to be printed, was drafted as 'Elinor & Marianne' in 1795 before being revised in 1797–8 into something like the published text of 1811. *Pride and Prejudice*—its world 'overset' (II.xvi) by militia movements responding to invasion threats from revolutionary France—was drafted as 'First Impressions' in 1796–7, and was the first novel submitted to a publisher. In one of the most egregious blunders in book-trade history, it was rejected out of hand by the generally astute Thomas Cadell ('declined by Return of Post', Cadell scrawled) and did not reach print until 1813. *Northanger Abbey* began life as 'Susan' in 1798–9, and in 1803 was the first novel to be sold, to a somewhat less upscale publisher named Benjamin Crosby (who, a decade earlier, had published *Caleb Williams*). Crosby advertised his acquisition as 'in the press', but failed to follow through, as Austen acidly recalled after buying back the manuscript in 1816: 'That any bookseller should think it worth while to purchase what he did not think it worth while to publish seems extraordinary' (*Northanger Abbey*, Advertisement).

Two conclusions may be drawn from this complex, agonizing history of composition, revision, and severely belated publication. The obvious point is that we must think of these three novels, though published in the 19th century, as being, in their creative inception, products of the 1790s. All were then revised or updated to an uncertain degree, but in the case of *Northanger Abbey*, Austen was quite explicit in asking readers to think of the text as representing an earlier world, since which time 'places, manners, books, and opinions have undergone considerable changes' (*Northanger Abbey*, Advertisement). The second point is that these novels were incremental processes, not instant products, and went through widely separated phases of revision as Austen reflected on prior drafts and considered the demands of a publishing world that seemed to be shutting her out. Moreover, just as *Northanger Abbey*, *Sense and Sensibility*, and *Pride and Prejudice* evolved over time into their final form, the incorporation into *Mansfield Park* and *Emma* of elements originating in 'The Watsons', an abandoned fragment of 1804, suggests a longer gestation for these works than is often assumed. It can be tempting to divide Austen's output into two discrete categories—three clever, self-conscious but callow experiments from her youth; then, after a fallow decade, three psychologically complex, technically flawless achievements of her maturity—but the reality is more fluid. In the words of the textual scholar Kathryn

Sutherland, narratives of development based on simple distinctions between 'early' and 'late' falsify Austen's practice. The publication period was merely 'the culmination of some twenty to thirty years of drafting, redrafting and continued experiment'.

Parodying the Gothic

Northanger Abbey is a rich and clever title, though it may have been settled on after Austen's death. Critics have unpacked its connotations: Catherine's precarious social status as a *hanger-on*, a dependant or even parasite; the volcanic *anger* of General Tilney when he perceives her that way. But the most obvious message concerns Gothic fiction. Like earlier satirical novels such as *The Female Quixote* (1752) by Charlotte Lennox (a book Austen read at least twice), *Northanger Abbey* reworks the classic premise of Cervantes in *Don Quixote* (1605–15), where a hero obsessed by chivalric romances comes to view the everyday world through their lens, and disastrously misinterprets his own lived experience. In Austen's first volume, set in the fashionable health resort of Bath, she binges on Gothic fiction from circulating libraries; in the second, her consciousness now dominated by Gothic tropes, she expects her visit to Northanger Abbey to match the pattern.

Abbeys held special allure in the Gothic repertoire, with the opportunities they offered for perverted religiosity and inquisitorial torment. Publications Austen may have known from circulating libraries include *Waldeck Abbey* (1795), *The Abbey of St Asaph* (1795), *Roach Abbey* (1796), *The Horrors of*

Oakendale Abbey (1797), and *Grasville Abbey* (1797); there were many more, up to and including Thomas Love Peacock's satirical *Nightmare Abbey* (1818). She neatly evokes the representational clichés common to these works when joking about her heroine's fanciful anticipation of Northanger. Approaching the General's home before night-fall, she's confident of sublime experience even so: 'every bend in the road was expected with solemn awe to afford a glimpse of its massy walls of grey stone, rising amidst a grove of ancient oaks, with the last beams of the sun playing in beautiful splendour on its high Gothic windows' (II.v). Her mind's eye reflects blood-curdling Minerva Press potboilers like Regina Maria Roche's *The Children of the Abbey* (1796), in which the heroine traverses oak-woods 'scattered over with relics of druidical antiquity'; she then admires from the 'massy door' of the abbey 'the dark and stupendous edifice, whose gloom was now heightened by the shadows of evening, with venerable awe'.

Here and elsewhere, Austen holds back from full-throttle parody, and in the chapters that follow, her comedy works through studiously downbeat descriptions of the mundane actualities of Northanger—the elegant, light-filled rooms, the consumer durables and modern comforts—that frustrate Catherine's novel-fuelled desires. Traces of captivating antiquity remain to be seen, like the pointed arches atop General Tilney's bright replacement windows, but the over-all impression is of rational modernity: swept gravel, even casements, pretty china. It all looks innocuous enough, and playfully at odds with the incongruous Gothic formulae— 'motionless with horror'; 'her blood was chilled' (II.vi)—that

Austen uses to evoke Catherine's feelings. These tags all sound very 1790s, which partly explains Austen's concern about her manuscript's best-before date as it languished with Crosby. Asked by Catherine if Northanger is 'a fine old place, just like what one reads about', Henry replies that they will not need to penetrate 'a hall dimly lighted by the expiring embers of a wood fire' (II.v). They will not encounter, in other words, the hackneyed thrills and off-the-peg shivers of Richard Warner's *Netley Abbey* (1795), where the hero, summoned into a gloomy refectory 'by screams of female distress', finds the villainous abbot creepily illuminated, as convention required, 'by the expiring embers of a large fire'.

Austen is not playing here, of course, on particular novels, but on their idiom in general. The exception is Radcliffe's *The Mysteries of Udolpho*, a reference point throughout *Northanger Abbey*, and a work that affords Catherine 'the luxury of a raised, restless, and frightened imagination' (I.vii) when she devours it on the instigation of Isabella, her fashion-victim friend. Even sophisticated Henry has read *Udolpho*, with, he jokes, his 'hair standing on end the whole time' (I.xiv). Creatively and commercially a peak of the genre (Radcliffe received £500 for the manuscript, fifty times more than Crosby paid Austen), *Udolpho* was celebrated especially for the character of Montoni, a brooding 16th-century brigand who starves his wife to death in a remote castle and immures the orphaned heroine there to gain control of her inheritance. It's this novel that dominates Catherine's imagination in Bath and sets up her torrid fantasies about Northanger, beguiling her mind from the

This attempt to describe the Effects of the Sublime & Wonderful is dedicated to M. G. Lewis Esqr MP

J. Gillray, inv & del

TALES of WONDER !

Figure 4 James Gillray, *Tales of Wonder!* (1802). The etching is ironically dedicated to the Gothic novelist and MP Matthew Lewis, whose spine-chilling *The Monk* (1796) mesmerizes a wealthy circle of fashion victims.

commonplace realities of civilized life in ways that will lead to humiliation.

Yet Austen quietly distinguishes between Radcliffe and her imitators when Catherine at last breaks loose from 'the visions of romance' (II.x). Her satirical target is not so much *Udolpho* as the torrent of clumsy replicas that followed in its wake—replicas such as the seven titles 'of the same kind' that Isabella lines up for Catherine to read next (I.vi), all actual publications of the 1790s (including even *Horrid Mysteries*, which sounds too good to be true). It's sometimes suggested, indeed, that *Northanger Abbey* is as much a tribute to *Udolpho* as a send-up of it, and that may also be true of less distinguished bone-chillers like *Netley Abbey*, with its 'screams of female distress'. For it turns out, on inspection, that Catherine has a good deal to scream about herself. Unlike Marianne, with her scarcely suppressed scream of agony in *Sense and Sensibility* (II.vii), she never quite lets it out, but there's a genuine sense in which the tyrannized heroines of these novels speak to her own condition in 1790s England. In this respect, Gothic fiction is not the end-point of Austen's satire in *Northanger Abbey*, but the means to a further end: an end that becomes visible when we recognize analogies as well as contrasts between Catherine's books and her world. At Bath and Northanger alike, her experience of that world is one of disempowerment and constraint, perhaps even tyranny or repression, for which the Gothic provides metaphors made no less eloquent by the wit of their handling.

Anxieties of common life

In a theory of parody advanced by the journalist William Hone just as *Northanger Abbey* came out, the mode could be divided into distinct categories. 'There were two kinds of parodies', Hone argued while being tried for blasphemous libel (he had parodied the liturgy): 'one in which a man might convey ludicrous or ridiculous ideas relative to some other subject; the other, where it was meant to ridicule the thing parodied.' A superficial account of *Northanger Abbey* would see it as a novel of female education that ridicules the thing parodied: Gothic fiction and the fashion for reading it. A naive, novel-obsessed heroine loses her grasp on reality, confuses a modern gentleman (General Tilney) with a Gothic villain, and is led out of her errors by a wise suitor (Henry). The cleverness of Austen's second volume lies in the mixed messages sent out about the General, but at one level he seems genial enough: not the Montoni of Catherine's imagination but a harmless retiree who delights in growing fruit and renovating the kitchen. By imagining him instead as the murderer of his wife, Catherine has entertained 'grossly injurious suspicions' inspired by her reading. But finally her mind is recalled from 'the alarms of romance' to encounter and recognize, free of distraction from bad literature, the sober and salutary 'anxieties of common life' (II.x).

Yet Austen uses Gothic fiction more ingeniously than this, and with something of Hone's outward movement. In the first place, although she enjoys sending up its more outré mannerisms, it's worth noting her refusal to denigrate it explicitly. She will not, like supercilious book reviewers, turn 'contemptuous censure' on pulp fiction (I.v). For while it may be absurd to take Gothic novels literally as a guide to modern life, these novels aren't necessarily absurd in themselves, and when more thoughtfully approached as metaphors of evil, they may have real explanatory power. After all, the polite world of a modern spa still has its perils and pains, and through clever deployment of Gothic hyperbole in her opening volume—Catherine repeatedly suffers 'dread', 'mortification', 'agony', 'misery', 'torment'—Austen draws quiet analogies between the trials of a Radcliffe heroine and the mundane but no less absorbing tribulations of an ingénue in predatory Bath. Catherine is manipulated and deceived by Isabella, and in effect abducted to Blaise Castle by boorish John Thorpe. She's constrained, even imprisoned, in a world of regulated proprieties (the rules of the ballroom, the conventions of the assembly), and cynically exploited by friends, or undeclared frenemies like Isabella, whose arm stays linked with hers 'though their hearts were at war' (I.xiii). Her predicament is not literally that of a Gothic novel. Yet Gothic novels can still express and reveal modes of persecution and entrapment that continue to operate, though in new guise, in a world of polite sociability.

In other ways the abortive trip to Blaise Castle, while in the first place indicating the phoniness of the Gothic craze, also conveys sinister implications of an up-to-the-minute kind, and in this respect anticipates the disquieting slavery theme of *Mansfield Park*. Antiquity and atmosphere are promised by John Thorpe, and his words arouse in Catherine thrilling fantasies of 'lofty rooms...for many years deserted' (I.xi). Yet as a good number of Austen's readers would have known, there was nothing authentic at all about Blaise Castle, an overblown exercise in cod medievalism that had been built as a folly by Thomas Farr, an 18th-century Bristol merchant whose wealth came from sugar and slaves. It's another of those moments at which Austen delicately associates the fashions and luxuries satirized in her fiction—the 'governess-trade' that worries Jane Fairfax (*Emma*, II.xvii); the opulence of Sir Thomas Bertram's estate—with the pressing offstage evil of Caribbean slavery. Even as Catherine's spine tingles at the thought of Blaise and its dungeons, Austen evokes the suffering not of medieval serfs but of modern slaves.

But what of autocratic, avaricious General Tilney? On the face of it, the speech in which Henry disabuses Catherine of her suspicions supports Austen's dry observation, a page or two later, that Gothic novels are no guide to life in 1790s England. Yet Henry's speech is also a masterpiece of double meaning on Austen's part, and he inadvertently implicates the General even as he seems to exonerate him on the surface (Box 2). The General may not literally have confined his fevered wife in a turret, like Radcliffe's Montoni, or starved her to death. To cut through Henry's apologies and evasions, however, is to see that he committed a more muted modern version of the same crime, imprisoning his wife in a loveless marriage ('We have not all...the same tenderness of disposition'), oppressing her in everyday life ('she...had much to bear'), and assailing her with irrational anger ('his temper injured her'). Perhaps there's even a meaningful sense in which General Tilney did indeed kill

---

BOX 2 *From* Northanger Abbey, *II.ix*

....

'Poor Eleanor *was* absent, and at such a distance as to return only to see her mother in her coffin.'

'But your father,' said Catherine, 'was *he* afflicted?'

'For a time, greatly so. You have erred in supposing him not attached to her. He loved her, I am persuaded, as well as it was possible for him to—We have not all, you know, the same tenderness of disposition—and I will not pretend to say that while she lived, she might not often have had much to bear, but though his temper injured her, his judgment never did. His value of her was sincere; and, if not permanently, he was truly afflicted by her death.'

'I am very glad of it,' said Catherine; 'it would have been very shocking!'—

'If I understand you rightly, you had formed a surmise of such horror as I have hardly words to—Dear Miss Morland, consider the dreadful nature of the suspicions you have entertained. What have you been judging from? Remember the country and the age in which we live. Remember that we are English, that we are Christians. Consult your own understanding, your own sense of the probable, your own observation of what is passing around you—Does our education prepare us for such atrocities? Do our laws connive at them? Could they be perpetrated without being known, in a country like this, where social and literary intercourse is on such a footing; where every man is surrounded by a neighbourhood of voluntary spies, and where roads and newspapers lay every thing open? Dearest Miss Morland, what ideas have you been admitting?'

They had reached the end of the gallery; and with tears of shame she ran off to her own room.

---

his long-suffering wife, or at least give her little to live for. It's hard not to be reminded, at any rate, of her merely transactional meaning to the General when Henry concludes, still with conspicuous unease, that 'his value of her was sincere; and, if not permanently, he was truly afflicted by her death' (II.ix). Austen has already told us about the value in net-worth terms of the former Miss Drummond, a wealthy heiress whose father had given her 'twenty thousand pounds, and five hundred to buy wedding-clothes' (I.ix). Happily for the General, the cash outlasts his grief. It continues to fund the little luxuries of Northanger Abbey— the fruit trees, the kitchen gadgets, the costly gilding—as surely as the labour of slaves funds Mansfield Park.

In this context, other things fall into place about General Tilney as the coercive, domineering authority figure of this very 1790s novel about fear. There's the inexplicably sinister atmosphere around him at Bath, for which surely '*he* could not be accountable' (II.i); the 'violence' and 'scolding' that alternate disconcertingly with his smiles at Northanger (II.vi); the aura of suppressed malignity from which Catherine eventually concludes 'that in suspecting General Tilney of either murdering or shutting up his wife, she had scarcely sinned against his character, or magnified his cruelty' (II.xv). More subliminal touches reinforce the sense of menace that Austen builds around the General, including the 'unquiet slumber' that Catherine suffers in his house (II.v), a phrase from *Richard III* that links him with Shakespeare's best-known murderous tyrant. He's certainly a latter-day Montoni, as he goes on to prove in his brutal expulsion of Catherine from Northanger—a clever reversal of Gothic convention by Austen (since heroines are normally walled in, not thrown out) that nonetheless reveals his essential affinity with Radcliffe's villain. Just as Montoni seeks to acquire the inheritance of *Udolpho*'s heroine, so the General seeks money and land—*more land*—from Catherine Morland, mistaking her for a second Miss Drummond.

It's fair to say in this context that reading Radcliffe has in the most important sense not misled Catherine at all; on the contrary, Radcliffe has trained her instincts to understand the General better than anyone else, including his son. The ideas she has been 'admitting' are close to the mark. Her one mistake has been to think of the Gothic as literally applicable to a modern world in which there is 'security for the existence even of a wife not beloved, in the laws of the land, and the manners of the age' (II.x). Conspicuously, Austen stops her list of securities for existence there, as though to imply that while laws and manners have changed, human nature has not, and has merely adjusted its methods to fit the times. Without the rather fragile infrastructure of modern society, with its newspapers and surveillance, unloved wives might still be killed, and unsuspecting heiresses robbed. And if the General, provincial patriarch and military man, in some ways stands in the novel for larger authority, the consequences look more alarming still. Evil has been domesticated, but the genteel world of Austen's satire still has its own quiet terrors.

3

Sense, Sensibility, Society

For the modernist author Rebecca West in 1932, Austen was not only familiar with Enlightenment feminism, specifically as it developed from broader 'rights of man' debate in the period. She was also its most incisive voice, however incongruous such an idea might seem. The intellectual ferment of the revolution era reached everywhere, West argued, into the conservative milieux of rural England as well as metropolitan radical circles. It needn't surprise us 'that a country gentlewoman should sit down and put the institutions of society regarding women through the most gruelling criticism they have ever received, just at the time when Europe was generally following Voltaire and Rousseau in their opinion that social institutions not only should but could be questioned'.

This is a startling claim to make about Austen, if only on the general grounds that novels tend to forfeit, with their characteristic complexity of representation and analysis, the polemical clarity of treatises or tracts: the clarity of works like, most obviously, Wollstonecraft's *Vindication of the Rights of Woman*, published a few years before Austen wrote her first versions of *Sense and Sensibility*, *Pride and Prejudice*, and *Northanger Abbey*. Fiction might richly, profoundly explore Wollstonecraft's themes—the mechanisms, assumptions, and practices that entrap women, from gendered norms of education and attainment to the laws of property transmission and marriage—but can it really subject these things to 'gruelling criticism'? West goes on to write insightfully about Austen's preference for indirection and implication over didacticism or controversy, and no doubt she knew this expression was a stretch. Yet her basic claim is not without substance, and since the rise of feminist scholarship in the later 20th century, much has been done to flesh it out with cultural-historical specificity and critical nuance. *Sense and Sensibility*, in which Austen explores the predicament of sisters (the 'Elinor & Marianne' of her working title) uprooted from comfortable lives and happy prospects by the terms of a great-uncle's will and the cupidity of its beneficiaries, has been central to the debate. Drafted and redrafted as the controversy provoked by the *Vindication* unfolded over the next few years, *Sense and Sensibility* addresses, alongside overtly radical novels of its day—Elizabeth Inchbald's *Nature and Art* (1796), Wollstonecraft's *The Wrongs of Woman* (1798), Mary Hays's *The Victim of Prejudice* (1799)—the precarious, dependent condition of unmoneyed women in a world of constraint and dispossession.

Precarity

Specificity about wealth, incomes, and the possibilities opened or foreclosed by money is a hallmark of Austen's fiction. But no other novel, with the possible exception of *Mansfield Park*, is quite so detailed at the outset about the financial and legal roots of its heroines' predicament. Raised in comfort at Norland, their great-uncle's large country estate, Elinor and Marianne (with their mother and sister) are abruptly tipped into genteel poverty by three circumstances, none disastrous in itself, but lethal to their prospects in combination. First, the nature of their great-uncle's bequest to their father, which stipulates that, subsequently, the estate be inherited intact by Elinor and Marianne's half-brother, John Dashwood; second, their father's early death, which prevents him securing their future over time with accumulated income from the estate; third, the moral feebleness of their half-brother, who vaguely plans to augment their small personal inheritance but is dissuaded by his grasping wife Fanny, one of the most gloriously atrocious characters in all Austen.

The death of the heroines' father is bad luck. But the other circumstances point to structural conditions that make female prosperity inherently precarious: in the first, the patriarchal impulse to concentrate property on a male heir, in this case the great-nephew, even when, Austen is emphatic, it's his half-sisters 'who most needed a provision' (I.i); in the third, a culture of acquisition, consumption, and display that turbocharges the greed of the John Dashwoods. For many 18th-century writers (Defoe is the conspicuous example), the word 'improvement' implies celebration of commercial morality and material progress. But in Austen's world, 'improvement' often carries an edge of vulgar ostentation and self-aggrandizement, at the expense of obligation to the community at large. In *Sense and Sensibility*, the point is deftly encapsulated when the John Dashwoods go on to build a gaudy new glass-house on the venerable Norland estate: 'The old walnut trees are all come down to make room for it', they brag (II.xi). They complain about what 'the inclosure of Norland Common' is costing them, without noting that this project—the privatization of previously public land, which would have required expensive lobbying in Parliament—will cost a great deal more to the local peasantry, now deprived of their customary rights to graze livestock, gather firewood, or hunt game on the common. Austen, as usual, leaves the consequence unspoken, but her readers would know the score.

For Elinor and Marianne, the further overarching circumstance is the unavailability of any realistic solution in their futures beyond securing a wealthy, landed, or otherwise flourishing husband. As Wollstonecraft points out in the *Vindication*, the prevailing system of female education has private or social accomplishment, not public or professional achievement, as its end goal, and 'the few employments open to women, so far from being liberal, are menial'. Even the role of governess is for Wollstonecraft a 'humiliating situation', alongside which 'nothing so painfully sharpens the sensibility as such a fall in life'. Austen's novels are not without the same apprehension, and in *Emma*, even polished Mrs Weston struggles to put her past role as a governess behind her: 'I was rather astonished to find her so very lady-like!' sneers dreadful Mrs Elton, always on the lookout for a sneaky put-down (II.xiv). A few chapters later in *Emma*, panic-stricken Jane Fairfax likens the prospect of becoming a governess to chattel slavery (see Chapter 5).

Victorian novelists such as George Eliot could write about female vocation as at least a meaningful ambition, but in the claustrophobic world of *Sense and Sensibility*, marriage is the only eligible destiny. In this respect, the courtship plot that structures all six of Austen's published novels, though sometimes held to imply her endorsement of a patriarchal status quo, is equally a means of exploring themes of female disempowerment. In *Sense and Sensibility*, both Elinor and Marianne fall in love, but in so doing they encounter further conditions that disadvantage them. First, the unshakeable predominance of social codes and courtship conventions that confer all agency on men, free to play the field and move on at will, and leave none for women, required to wait decorously and patiently for proposals, prone to recurrent anxiety and disappointment, but forbidden from taking initiatives of their own, despite the higher stakes arising from their situation. Then there's the fecklessness—enabled by these codes and the power imbalance they cement—of the unreliable suitors concerned: in Marianne's case, philandering Willoughby, with his rakish back catalogue of seduction and betrayal; in Elinor's, two-timing Edward Ferrars, a virtuoso of mixed messages and self-pity. *Pride and Prejudice* is the explicit model for one of the cleverest modern reworkings of Austen, Helen Fielding's *Bridget Jones's Diary* (1996). But at the start of Bridget's diary, her resolution not to fall this year for 'commitment phobics, people with girlfriends or wives, misogynists, megalomaniacs, chauvinists, emotional fuckwits or freeloaders' has more than a whiff of *Sense and Sensibility* about it.

Feeling

To one of the novel's first reviewers, *Sense and Sensibility* was something like a fictionalized conduct manual, and could instruct readers confronting similar trials in the necessary do's and don'ts (Box 3). Sobriety, fortitude, self-command: these are the virtues flowing from sense; unregulated emotionalism is the countervailing, and potentially catastrophic, vice of sensibility. Novels like that were certainly around when Austen drafted 'Elinor & Marianne' in the 1790s, full of giddy, self-indulgent sentimentalists and upright exemplars of proper decorum. So there were again when she published *Sense and Sensibility* in 1811, and it's sometimes argued that Austen broke into print by melting into the generic background as opposed to asserting her difference. With its focus on female experience and emotion, and the struggles of young women against romantic obstacles and social conventions, her novel fluently repeats the popular, marketable routines of courtship fiction. This is the genre that flies from the shelves in graphic satires of the period about circulating libraries (see Figure 5, the sermons in place, the novels gone), its sympathetic heroines beleaguered by, or successfully domesticating, glamorous rakes.

For Deidre Lynch, *Sense and Sensibility* has subtleties and surprises all of its own, but on the surface 'indulges novel readers with the pleasures of instant legibility—the pleasure of character *types*'. Lynch points out the overlapping language of mechanized printing and formula fiction (the terms 'stereotype' and 'cliché' were both coined in Austen's

BOX 3 *From the* British Critic *(May 1812), 527*

The object of the work is to represent the effects on the conduct of life, of discreet quiet good sense on the one hand, and an over-refined and excessive susceptibility on the other. The characters are happily delineated and admirably sustained. Two sisters are placed before the reader, similarly circumstanced in point of education and accomplishments, exposed to similar trials, but the one by a sober exertion of prudence and judgment sustains with fortitude, and overcomes with success, what plunges the other into an abyss of vexation, sorrow, and disappointment. An intimate knowledge of life and of the female character is exemplified in the various personages and incidents which are introduced, and nothing can be more happily pourtrayed than the picture of the elder brother, who required by his dying father, to assist his mother and sisters, first resolves to give the sisters a thousand pounds a-piece, but after a certain deliberation with himself, and dialogue with his *amiable* wife, persuades himself that a little fish and game occasionally sent, will fulfil the real intentions of his father, and satisfy every obligation of duty. Not less excellent is the picture of the young lady of over exquisite sensibility, who falls immediately and violently in love with a male coquet, without listening to the judicious expostulations of her sensible sister, and believing it impossible for man to be fickle, false, and treacherous. We will, however, detain our female friends no longer than to assure them, that they may peruse these volumes not only with satisfaction but with real benefit, for they may learn from them, if they please, many sober and salutary maxims for the conduct of life, exemplified in a very pleasing and entertaining narrative.

Figure 5 *The Circulating Library* (1804). A genteel patron peruses the catalogue, hoping to borrow sentimental titles (*Man of Feeling*; *Cruel Disappointment*; *Reuben, or Suicide*) and spurning didactic alternatives (*True Delicacy*; *School of Virtue*; *Test of Filial Duty*).

day to denote new print technologies), but she also sees Austen as endowing the stock characters from which she begins with complex new impressions of inward life. Pitting rounded characters against flat, and working with a familiar contrast between exemplars of right and wrong conduct, *Sense and Sensibility* breaks fresh ground in its representation of human consciousness, while at the same time offering readers surface patterns and moral binaries they had encountered elsewhere.

On the side of sensibility in particular, Austen's novel also explores one of the most prominent themes of Wollstonecraft's *Vindication*. A generation beforehand, the capacity to feel was routinely celebrated in a school of thought, sometimes labelled sentimentalism, that involved several strands: an elevation of benevolence as the primary human virtue, seen as arising from sympathetic fellow-feeling and as issuing in philanthropic action; an assumption that such impulses are innate, inherently the possession of a species characterized by mutual affection and sociable good nature; a willingness to cultivate instead of repress the tender passions, as the source of not only virtuous conduct but also pleasurable self-approval. When the philosopher David Hume wrote that 'morality . . . is more properly felt than judg'd of ', or again that moral ideas are instilled not by argument or induction but 'by an immediate feeling and finer internal sense', he gave intellectual rigour to a style of thinking most famously pursued by Adam Smith in his *Theory of Moral Sentiments* (1759).

There were numerous sources of backlash in Wollstonecraft's day, but her own distinctive objection concerned the association between feeling and passive femininity, and, for women, the debilitating consequences of sensibility as a compulsory attainment. In practice, a culture that supposed 'weak elegancy of mind, exquisite sensibility, and sweet docility of manners . . . to be the sexual characteristics of the weaker vessel' had the inevitable effect of enslaving women, depriving them of firmness or strength, and rendering them vulnerable to exploitation. Systems of education and social expectation turned them, potentially the equals of men, into helpless subordinates: 'Their senses are inflamed, and their understandings neglected; consequently they become the prey of their senses, delicately termed sensibility, and are blown about by every momentary gust of feeling.' In her novel *The Wrongs of Woman*, Wollstonecraft goes on to dramatize this view of feeling and its cult, most of all when enshrined in fiction, as luring female readers into a state of 'intoxicated sensibility'. It foists on them a debilitating image of themselves as 'only born to feel'.

Austen is never Wollstonecraft, and never a dealer in polemic or strident critique. But she shares Wollstonecraft's interest in the downside of feeling, and in the role of fiction, and literature more broadly, in promoting the cult of sensibility. By comparison with the Catherine of *Northanger Abbey*, we hear a good deal less about what Marianne consumes as a reader. But even when poetry rather than fiction is specified, her reading associates her firmly with the novel of sensibility, a genre characterized by overwrought representations of emotion, and underpinned by an ethics in which feeling displaces reason or duty as the highest mark of personal worth. Marianne is a devotee of the poet William Cowper, we soon learn (I.iii), and this detail not only aligns her with sentimental types like the tremulous heroine of Elizabeth Isabella Spence's *Helen Sinclair* (1799), whose favourite recreation is to stroll in the woods with her lover and a copy of Cowper, which they read with emotion beyond expression ('a look of intelligence spoke how much they felt'). Marianne's choice also recalls Cowper's valorization of sympathetic feeling over worldly reason: 'I would not enter on my list of friends | (Though graced with polish'd manners and fine sense | Yet wanting sensibility) the man | Who needlessly sets foot upon a worm.' Austen admired Cowper herself, but she also laughed at his excesses.

Like Catherine with her novels of terror, moreover, Marianne approaches daily experience as a lived-out novel of sensibility. When Colonel Brandon starts but then abruptly drops a story about female ruin (with Willoughby the unnamed culprit), Elinor senses how Marianne's imagination would have novelized the story 'in the most melancholy order of disastrous love' (I.xi). Romantically rescued by Willoughby from the rain-lashed hills, her immediate response is to find 'his person and air . . . equal to what her fancy had ever drawn for the hero of a favourite story' (I.ix). This particular mistake is excusable enough, since Austen gives much of her plot a teasing resemblance to the genre of sentimental fiction. A magazine tale has even been uncovered ('The Shipwreck', in the *Lady's Magazine* for 1794), in which the heroine, one Miss Brandon, finds love when saved from drowning by a dashing stranger named Willoughby.

In the somewhat dispiriting final chapter of *Sense and Sensibility*, however, Marianne is disabused. In learning to love unglamorous Colonel Brandon, she's forced to recognize that assumptions drawn from her favourite genre—the assumption, in particular, that broken-hearted lovers can never love again—don't match real-world experience. Where Catherine finds that modern life isn't literally a Gothic novel, Marianne thus finds that it isn't a novel of sensibility either. In such a novel, strictly speaking, a heroine like herself would have fallen 'a sacrifice to an irresistible passion, as once she had fondly flattered herself with expecting' (III.xiv). Instead, she's led 'to discover the falsehood of her own opinions', and to contradict them in practice. Moreover, Austen adds by way of authorial comment, any assumption that a penitent Willoughby will have fallen in with generic norms and 'died of a broken heart, must not be depended on' (III.xiv). His real-world heart is far too flexible to get itself broken.

If *Sense and Sensibility* refuses to conform to the lineaments of a sentimental novel, however, in other ways it bears comparison with a different fictional type. The late 18th-century critique of sensibility—which came not only from radicals like Wollstonecraft, for whom feeling enfeebled its devotees, but also conservatives like Hannah More, for whom it usurped more solid religious duties—also spilled over into fiction. In novels with titles like *Excessive Sensibility* (1787) and *The Errors of Sensibility* (1793), conditions of extreme emotion start to look like delusions or snares. In *Arulia; or, The Victim of Sensibility* (1790) and *Infidelity; or, The Victims of Sentiment* (1797), the cherished virtue of refined feeling, far from alleviating distress, becomes its main cause.

For other novelists of sensibility, it was business as usual for some while longer, and their output remained a live target not only for Austen but also for lesser-known rivals. Eaton Stannard Barrett's *The Heroine* (1813), which Austen thought 'a delightful burlesque' (2 March 1814), repudiates sentimental fiction as making its readers 'admire ideal scenes of transport and distraction; and feel disgusted with the vulgarities of living misery'. But anti-sentimental fiction was already well established in the 1790s. Didactic contrast novels like Maria Edgeworth's *Letters of Julia and Caroline* (1795) and Jane West's *A Gossip's Story* (1796) juxtaposed the attitudes and adventures of contrasting protagonists, typically proposing one as a model of resolute virtue, the other as a warning against disabling feeling. In one of the most influential modern interpretations of *Sense and Sensibility*, this is precisely the mould in which Austen casts the novel. Though occasionally sensing authorial impatience with the structural and moral rigidity of the contrast schema, Marilyn Butler argues that Austen 'conscientiously maintains the principle of a didactic comparison...The entire action is organized to represent Elinor and Marianne in terms of rival value-systems.'

Self-command

It's certainly not hard to detect a pattern in which Marianne's extravagant demonstrations of feeling are unfavourably contrasted with Elinor's emotional control and commitment to rational propriety. From the opening chapter of a narrative that is typically (though not always) presented through Elinor's perspective, we witness her concern at 'the excess of her sister's sensibility' (I.i). Throughout the novel, Marianne is depicted in terms of an established fictional repertoire of faints, fits, and fevers, and she repeats the postures and gestures of countless sentimental heroines before her. Abandoned by the capricious Willoughby, she falls into 'a silent agony, too much oppressed even for tears' (II.vi); she then composes the obligatory epistolary *cri de coeur*, 'writing as fast as a continual flow of tears would permit her' (II.vii). Meanwhile, confronted with comparable trials from her differently unsuitable lover, Elinor exerts herself to maintain appearances of fortitude and poise, exemplary in her unruffled manner, dry eyes, and measured, undemonstrative language.

The most obvious characteristic shared by Austen's protagonists is a helpful habit of drawing explicit contrasts between one another: 'you, because you communicate, and I, because I conceal nothing', as Marianne spells it out at one point (II.v). But in other respects they seem entirely different in attitude and conduct. The difference is dramatized as well as explained, nowhere more effectively than in their different styles of appearing at dinner in the immediate wake of emotional crisis. Following Willoughby's first snub, Marianne is swollen-eyed and unable to speak, and eventually bursts into tears and leaves the room. There's a sense, moreover, in which she does so from perverse principle, not just uncontrolled emotion, dominated as her thinking is by novelistic models of extreme sensibility. 'She was without any power, because she was without any desire of command over herself' (I.xv), and in the night to follow 'would have thought herself very inexcusable had she been able to sleep at all' (I.xvi).

Where Marianne thinks composure a disgrace, Elinor works obsessively in the same situation at self-command, that stoical virtue which, for Adam Smith, was a constantly needed check on the passions and feelings. It's also a virtue that Wollstonecraft promotes in contradistinction to the vice of excessive sensibility, though she tends to use alternative terms like 'fortitude', 'strength of mind', and 'steadiness of conduct'. In Austen's novel, self-command is a discipline Elinor rehearses with care, urges on her sister, and on one occasion even enlists for the sake of deceiving her hard-nosed rival Lucy Steele. On another occasion, learning of Lucy's engagement to the man she took to be her own suitor, 'Elinor's security sunk; but her self-command did not sink with it' (I.xxii). By the same token, 'composure of mind' is for the elder sister a hard-won but all-important achievement, 'the effect of constant and painful exertion' (III.i).

Even so, just as there's audible mockery of Marianne in Austen's account of her determination to be unable to sleep, there seems something less than full approval, and a sense of almost inhuman self-denial, in her later account of Elinor's inscrutable, unshaken demeanour when arriving at dinner 'two hours after she had first suffered the extinction of all her dearest hopes' (II.i). At such moments, the contrast between sensibility and sense, extravagant emotionalism and strenuous self-discipline, seems clear enough. But is this a straightforward contrast between wrong and right? Or is 'the self-command she had practised since her first know-ledge of Edward's engagement' (III.i) instead a quality that makes Elinor complicit in her own suffering, by enabling others to wrong her with confidence that no one will know?

As critics of the contrast-novel theory have often main-tained, there are good reasons to pause before seeing *Sense and Sensibility* as an unequivocal replication, as opposed to a subtle complication, of the polarized absolutes of didactic fiction. In the first place, it's by no means self-evident that the talismanic words in Austen's title, which after all are cognate terms, should be understood in binary opposition. In figures such as Colonel Brandon—'undoubtedly a sens-ible man' (III.iv)—the two qualities coalesce into a harmo-nious, albeit somewhat unprepossessing, amalgam of feeling and reason. Another way of reading the title would be by analogy with *Pride and Prejudice*, which explores over-lapping, interweaving characteristics, not a clash of simple opposites. For every novel of the period in which 'sense' and 'sensibility' are antithetical terms, furthermore, another rec-ognizes their congruence. In Elizabeth Gunning's *The Orphans of Snowdon* (1797), the sorrowing heroine attempts, without quite attaining, 'the victory of sense over sensibil-ity'. But in Isabella Kelly's *The Abbey of St Asaph* (1795), the heroine (named Elinor) is introduced with 'all the mild virtues beaming in her eyes, while sense and sensibility animated her charming features'. This novel later compli-ments another character for her ability to console the dis-tressed with reason and feeling operating in tandem: 'your sense would direct, and your sensibility sooth me'.

Plenty of indications in Austen's novel suggest that her interest is not only in contrasting the sense of one sister with the sensibility of the other—'the same steady conviction and affectionate counsel on Elinor's side, the same impetuous feelings and varying opinions on Marianne's' (II.ix)—regular and emphatic though these contrasts are. Her ambiguous use of the adjective 'sensible' (possessing either sense, or sensibility, or both) looks calculated to confuse the issue, so that Marianne is 'sensible and clever' when credited with Elinor-like 'sense' in the opening chapter (I.i), while Elinor is later 'feelingly sensible' in Marianne's manner, afflicted by 'emotion and distress beyond any thing she had ever felt before' (I.xxii). A properly flexible account of *Sense and Sensibility* would see it as a novel in which simple binaries break down, with Elinor learning the legitimacy of feeling and Marianne attempting self-command. As the narrative progresses, Austen reaches points at which the rational sister can be praised for a 'strongly felt' emotion (III.iii), the emotional one for showing 'resolute composure' (II.x).

Yet even if one accepts that *Sense and Sensibility* is a novel of antithetical characters and characteristics, it's by no means self-evident that the 'sensibility' side of the equation is entirely rejected. Like *Northanger Abbey*, turning as it does on the subjection of Miss Morland (and before her Miss Drummond) to mercenary wooing, *Sense and Sensibility* is a novel about exploitation, and exploitation in a variety of senses, emotional and social as well as economic. Back stories are used to reinforce the theme, like Brandon's tale of a relative coerced into marriage because 'her fortune was large, and our family estate much encumbered' (II.ix), and it suffuses the main plot. Strict patrilineal inheritance leaves Elinor and Marianne financially vulnerable, and the attrition is compounded by their brother's monstrous wife, a one-woman Goneril-and-Regan show ('They will have no carriage, no horses, and hardly any servants', I.ii), who knocks them to the lowest rung of their social world. From this predicament marriage is the only escape, yet here too the deck is stacked against them by custom and convention, in particular by proprieties of courtship that confer all agency and power on their callous suitors—an effect intensified by further meddling from malicious Fanny Dashwood.

In this context, Elinor's refusal to turn a hair two hours after the extinction of her hopes implies not only robotic repression but also an acquiescence in codes of behaviour that work to entrap her. By contrast, Marianne's habit of causing stirs and making scenes, while at one level a mark of culpable self-absorption, also serves to disrupt social mechanisms that empower rank, wealth, and especially masculinity at the expense of both sisters. In this sense, histrionics are her only available means of registering protest or fighting back. At times, there looks to be something rather knowing about Marianne's violation of the behavioural proprieties on which the whole system depends, as when she acknowledges having 'erred against every common-place notion of decorum . . . where I ought to have been reserved, spiritless, dull, and deceitful' (I.x). At others, her attacks on cold-eyed pragmatism in society are more than mere effusions of unworldly sensibility. Given the numerous bad matches in *Sense and Sensibility* (witness Mr Palmer, embittered because physical attraction has made him 'the husband of a very silly woman' (I.xx)), she sounds cogent and compelling when insisting that marriage must be for love. It would otherwise be merely transactional: 'a compact of convenience...a commercial exchange, in which each wished to be benefited at the expense of the other' (I.viii).

Here Marianne pinpoints that pervasive theme in Austen which for the poet W. H. Auden in 1937 made James Joyce, author of *Ulysses*, seem comparatively 'innocent as grass': money, and the social institutions—marriage, inheritance, family—that serve to accumulate, protect, and transmit it. Her most disconcerting ability, Auden writes in playfully Marxian terms, is to

> Describe the amorous effect of 'brass',
> Reveal so frankly and with such sobriety
> The economic basis of society.

It's a less serious claim than Rebecca West's about the institutions of society regarding women, and more aptly worded ('describe' and 'reveal' as opposed to 'gruelling criticism'), since Austen's method is much more about showing than telling. She represents and satirizes, but doesn't theorize. And while the novels unmistakably portray a world ordered by formal and informal systems of rules, they do so in an older language: Austen writes about manners and morals, not social institutions, and 'society' means in her usage a circle of acquaintance or the company of others, not anything larger or more abstract.

At the same time, the resources of fiction gave Austen a uniquely powerful perspective on the forces and conditions that hem in a character such as Marianne, who then rebels against them to dramatic effect. Marianne is far more at such moments than a vehicle for satire on novels of sensibility, and she at once demonstrates and articulates an element of social critique in Austen that is no less real for being subtle and indirect. As Catherine Morland in her Gothic delusions gets the mercenary master of Northanger Abbey more or less right, so Marianne in her sentimental histrionics finds the most powerful answer possible to a world of exploitative Willoughbys and calculating Fanny Dashwoods. In a startling disruption of a rule-bound world, she 'almost screamed with agony' (II.vii), and the agony comes to haunt even Willoughby himself—'Marianne's sweet face as white as death' (III.viii)—as he drives through the night to seek atonement. As William Empson writes in his classic essay on *Sense and Sensibility*, 'it is a detail that you might get in Dostoevsky'.

4

The Voices of *Pride and Prejudice*

The brilliance of *Pride and Prejudice* has many aspects, but fundamental to all of them is its narrative economy and restraint. Austen probably intensified this feature in late revision, since when trying to sell 'First Impressions' in the 1790s, her father compared it in length to Frances Burney's hugely successful *Evelina* (*c.*155,000 words), though *Pride and Prejudice* as published in 1813 was a good deal shorter (*c.*122,000 words). Writing to her sister, Austen talked of having 'lopt & cropt' her text, like an arborist pruning excess growth for the sake of form (29 January 1813). Inquits (speech tags) to guide readers through her characters' conversations were among the casualties of the process, and Austen acknowledged that in the published version 'a "said he" or a "said she" would sometimes make the Dialogue more immediately clear'. The gain in pace offsets any loss of clarity, however. As E. M. Forster wrote of one such moment in *Pride and Prejudice*, 'the dialogue lights up and sends a little spark of fire into the main mass of the novel'.

Austen was more tongue-in-cheek when blaming herself for failing to work in irrelevant padding like other novelists: 'an Essay on Writing, a critique on Walter Scott, or the history of Buonaparté—or anything that would form a contrast & bring the reader with increased delight to the playfulness & Epigrammatism of the general stile' (4 February 1813). A minimalist aesthetic was always Austen's governing principle, and it was in this spirit that she urged a would-be novelist among her nieces to pare back narrative redundancy and leave realist detail to be supplied by the reader's imagination. Her niece's descriptions of place and gesture were too minute: 'You give too many particulars of right hand & left' (9 September 1814). It was voice that mattered above all in Austen's art, and it's in *Pride and Prejudice*, a masterpiece of less-is-more narration, that this pioneering aspect of her achievement is most clearly seen.

Epigram

With 'Call me Ishmael' (*Moby Dick*), 'It was the best of times' (*A Tale of Two Cities*), and 'All happy families are alike' (*Anna Karenina*), the first line of *Pride and Prejudice* makes one of the best-known opening gambits in all fiction: 'It is a truth universally acknowledged, that a single man in possession of a good fortune, must be in want of a wife' (I.i). Yet this is also, as soon as we stop and think about it, a somewhat perplexing line. Whose voice and views are we listening to here, what status or value should we grant them, and what does the author think? In its confident declarative style, the line—indeed the paragraph, for Austen leaves it at that—seems to promise direct access to authorial opinion. It adopts a standard formula from polemical writing of the period to mark moments of special emphasis, inflated from subjective assertion into absolute truth. In practice, a sceptical reader might question that truth, but the author's commitment to it can't be mistaken.

In Austen's hands, however, the rhetorical flourish is punctured by the parochialism of its content. For there's nothing remotely universal about this particular truth, and in another time or place, a single man in possession of a good fortune might just as well want (lack, with a connotation of desire) a shady accountant, a casual fling, or a husband. The timeless present-tense mode notwithstanding, Austen is telling us not about universal truth at all, but about a socially and historically specific set of attitudes. In ways made inescapable as the novel unfolds, her statement suggests not reliable authorial truth-telling—the wise, moralizing commentary that guides readers through George Eliot's *Middlemarch*, say—but satirical invocation of a communal voice. It conjures up the shared perspective of genteel home-counties society—'the minds of the surrounding families' (I.i)—and mimics the thought and language of this society: diminished thought and impoverished language, in which the petty, self-interested assumptions of Mrs Bennet and her neighbours are casually dignified into something more. A masterstroke of comic bathos and teasing plot anticipation, the trick also foreshadows the clever intricacies, strategic uncertainties, and subtle, agile ventriloquisms of the narrative ahead.

Letters

A standard explanation for Austen's virtuoso handling of narrative voice in *Pride and Prejudice,* and *Sense and Sensibility* before it, is that key features of her technique originate in the tradition of epistolary fiction. More than a century before Austen drafted either novel, Aphra Behn's ground-breaking *Love-Letters between a Nobleman and His Sister* (1684–7) used letters to highlight the viewpoint of its characters, and in Austen's youth this method was still being refined in works like *Evelina* (1778) and the masterpiece of the genre in French, *Les Liaisons dangereuses* (1782) by Choderlos de Laclos. The major British epistolary novelist was Samuel Richardson, who used terms like 'writing to the moment' and 'writing from the heart' to suggest the immediacy and intimacy associated with letter fiction: first, its dramatic synchronization of story and discourse, with narrators reacting to events as they unfold; second, the psychological transparency of unguarded, spontaneous missives to close friends. In Richardson's hands, the novel in letters also produces more complex effects, above all in his multi-voiced *Clarissa* (1747–8), where competing narrators advance rival accounts of the underlying story, its causes and effects, its rights and wrongs. In Laclos, letters become agents of deception and betrayal, not vehicles of reliable information. *Les Liaisons dangereuses* dramatizes a struggle for power—war, one narrator finally calls it—that plays out in the epistolary medium itself.

In 1787, the year Austen began satirizing epistolary conventions in her juvenilia, half the new novels published in

English—24 of 47—were told in letters. Yet the numbers mask a creative decline, and with occasional exceptions there was little more to the epistolary novels that crowded the market than vapid, lumbering imitation of Richardson's last and then most influential work, his voluminous novel of manners *Sir Charles Grandison* (1753–4). Youthful skits such as 'Love and Freindship', 'Lesley Castle', and 'A Collection of Letters' deftly mock the sentimental excesses and creaking mechanics of this persistent strain of circulating-library fiction, but Austen's admiration for the towering prototype is very clear. Family memoirs report her absorption in the circumstantial detail and meticulous characterization of *Grandison*, and her unrivalled knowledge of Richardson's work overall.

The family would not have made the same claim about scandalous Laclos. But in her longest surviving exercise in epistolary fiction, the astonishing 'Lady Susan' (composed *c.*1794), Austen is fascinated by letters as agents of duplicity and manipulation, not vehicles of documentary realism or tokens of the inner life. Daringly, and in marked contrast to the published novels, the heroine of 'Lady Susan' is a scheming adulteress, and the novel may be indebted to the widely publicized adultery trials and divorce scandals of the era. Yet Lady Susan is at the same time glamorous, exuberant, and winning, while the decent, respectable characters around her come across as plodding dupes. It's an effect unnervingly close to Machiavelli, but closest of all to Laclos. The work employs multiple narrators, some of them uncomprehending, but Lady Susan herself is the primary voice: a voice marked above all by her ability to beguile, and to beguile specifically as a letter-writer, exerting 'a happy command of Language, which is too often used I beleive to make Black appear White' (letter vi). Rather than describe the 'captivating Deceit' (letter iv) of this transgressive character in clear, objective narration, 'Lady Susan' exposes readers directly to her deceitful writing, unassisted—until a short third-person 'Conclusion', probably added in 1805—by any guidance from a detached voice. The work becomes a minor masterpiece of 'epistolarity' in the sense established by the narrative theorist Janet Altman: 'the use of the letter's formal properties to create meaning'.

Other works from this key period of Austen's creativity do not survive, or survive only in the form of radical rewrites. *Pride and Prejudice*, *Sense and Sensibility*, and *Northanger Abbey* all originate in drafts composed by Austen in her early twenties, and beyond the working titles (respectively 'First Impressions', 'Elinor & Marianne', 'Susan') we know little for sure about these drafts. It's widely accepted, however, that at least one was epistolary. 'Memory is treacherous', confessed Austen's niece Caroline decades later, 'but I cannot be mistaken in saying that Sense and Sensibility was *first* written in letters.' However, the residually epistolary aspect of *Sense and Sensibility* isn't pronounced, and structural considerations (Elinor and Marianne are rarely apart; they lack appropriate addressees elsewhere) make it hard to see the trace of a novel in letters. Some scholars have suggested—since memory is treacherous indeed, and Caroline wasn't born until 1805—that a more plausible candidate is *Pride and Prejudice*, which turns on letters as narrative vehicles or agents of plot at key junctures, and has nearly five times as much epistolary content as *Sense and Sensibility*. We need only remember the pivotal explanation of himself that Mr Darcy hands Elizabeth in the grove near Rosings, the toe-curling, self-promoting letters of Mr Collins, or the epistolary mediation of the Lydia–Wickham subplot, to see how central letters are to the comic and dramatic effects of *Pride and Prejudice*. Especially, letters animate the patterns of self-revelation, delayed disclosure, and ongoing assessment of character and action that drive the work.

Perhaps that's why George Austen's mind turned to *Evelina*, the best-known novel in letters of the previous generation, as he tried to tempt a publisher with 'First Impressions'. That said, Burney's novel does little to exploit epistolary fiction's potential to diversify narrative perspectives, and her typical heading for each letter is 'Evelina in continuation'. By contrast, *Pride and Prejudice* develops a finely calibrated range of epistolary voices, which shift according to situation and addressee as well as from writer to writer ('idiolect' is a term sometimes used for the character-specific patterns of speech that Austen fashions with such fine-tuned consistency). At first sight, in achieving this effect, she seems to stick with the basic convention of epistolary immediacy, where letters are transparent windows on authentic selves. The unguarded openness of Mr Bingley's epistolary style—'rapidity of thought and carelessness of execution' (I.x)—is emphasized early on, and writing from the heart is always the governing assumption with guileless Jane, whose letters 'prove what she felt' (II.iii). Yet even these letters can't be taken at face value. Darcy challenges Bingley's artlessness as merely a pose; Elizabeth scrutinizes Jane's words for tell-tale signs of undeclared feeling. No less important than the writing of letters is the vigilant reading of letters, which are always more or less than pure inwardness. They yield up their full meaning only when read with the patience that Elizabeth bestows on Jane's, re-perusing them for hidden messages, and dwelling on their local evasions.

It's tempting to see in this sisterly correspondence, which culminates in Jane's breathless report of Lydia's elopement, the trace of a fully epistolary 'First Impressions', and there may be another in the correspondence Elizabeth maintains with Charlotte after Charlotte marries slimy Mr Collins and moves to Kent. The separation of the heroine from one confidante or the other for most of the action suggests, as *Sense and Sensibility* never does, the structural preconditions of a novel in letters. If so, however, Austen was writing epistolary narrative of a complex, unreliable kind, requiring that it be read between the lines for lapses in candour, or assessed in light of distortions particular to each narrator. Charlotte's marriage makes her a guarded, self-censoring writer whose letters display nothing more genuine than a 'rationally softened' version of Mr Collins's skewed viewpoint (II.iii). Jane is a deficient narrator not only from personal reticence but also from her trusting nature, as Elizabeth notes of her letter describing caddish Mr Wickham's honourable intentions.

Elsewhere Austen seems interested in correspondence not as a vehicle of dramatic representation or psychological outpour but as a medium of cool deception or covert attack.

Witness the 'high flown expressions' of sneering Miss Bingley's letters to Jane, which Elizabeth assesses 'with all the insensibility of distrust' (I.xxi), or Collins's knife-twisting letter of condolence on Lydia's disgrace (III.vi), inserted with tension-snapping comic timing that rivals the porter scene in *Macbeth*. The need to treat letters as a slippery, inherently untrustworthy medium, always to be analysed or decoded with care, is nowhere more fully registered than in a chapter devoted to Elizabeth's obsessive, fluctuating reading of Darcy's letter of explanation, during which 'she studied every sentence: and her feelings towards its writer were at times widely different' (III.viii). In attempting to undo the damage of his botched proposal, this carefully meditated letter is among the most significant and enigmatic utterances in the book. This letter still reverberates in the closing chapters: '"Did it," said he, "did it *soon* make you think better of me?"' (III.xvi).

Authority

Yet for all Austen's attraction to letters, if not as reliable narration or unstudied self-portraiture then as interpretative challenges for both characters and readers, *Pride and Prejudice* also shows frustration with the technique. When Bingley as letter-writer thinks it 'too much, to remember at night all the foolish things that were said in the morning' (I.x), he echoes a long-standing objection to epistolary novels as bloated by redundant detail and baggy prolixity. Objections like this intensified during Austen's lifetime, and despite its ongoing currency with circulating-library audiences, the novel in letters was increasingly disparaged or discarded by leading writers. Burney dropped the mode after *Evelina*, and it's her non-epistolary fiction that Austen praises in *Northanger Abbey*. Walter Scott, the most prestigious novelist in English by the time Austen died, abandons letter-narrative part-way through *Redgauntlet* (1824), citing its lack of provision for authorial guidance. Even multi-voiced epistolary fiction cannot 'contain all in which it is necessary to instruct the reader for his full comprehension of the story'.

The clunky infrastructure and rhetorical constraints of epistolary fiction also underlie Austen's farewell to the mode in her third-person 'Conclusion' to 'Lady Susan'. In her playful declaration that the correspondence, 'by a meeting between some of the Parties & a separation between the others, could not, to the great detriment of the Post office Revenue, be continued longer', one hears emerge the assured, urbane voice of the mature novels, decisively intervening to clarify and resolve. No longer is the kinship with Richardson; instead, Austen approaches the witty, managerial tones of Richardson's great antagonist Henry Fielding. In particular, she recalls a sly comment by Fielding in *Joseph Andrews* (1742), which could not be epistolary for an insurmountable reason, 'and this was, that poor *Fanny* [the heroine] could neither write nor read'.

It's a commonplace of literary history that Austen's breakthrough achievement was to meld the contrasting techniques of Richardson and Fielding into a flexible third-person mode that also conveyed the authentic intimacy of first-person introspection. Yet Austen never quite discards the ostentatious artifice of Fielding's practice, notably his fondness for disrupting the illusion of natural narrative with self-conscious reminders of authorial shaping. *Pride and Prejudice* contains no frame-breaking gesture as overt as Austen's joke about the 'tell-tale compression of the pages' signalling the imminent happy ending of *Northanger Abbey* (II.xvi). Yet several passages come close to this, like Austen's emphatic authorial judgement about Mrs Bennet in the final chapter, when 'I wish I could say', she writes with a weary shake of the head, that events in the novel 'produced so happy an effect as to make her a sensible, amiable, well-informed woman for the rest of her life' (III.xix). The scarcity of these first-person intrusions makes them all the more emphatic.

For critics who prize Austen as a pioneer of free indirect style (see below), comments like this are blemishes in a method to be celebrated for eliminating authorial personality. In one influential statement (by Roy Pascal), Austen creates a narrator 'who is (with rare lapses) non-personal, non-defined, and therefore may enjoy access to the most secret privacy of the characters'. Yet these 'lapses' were a key part of Austen's repertoire, and though she never embraces authorial first person with the insistence of Fielding, neither does she discard this technique completely. In their eagerness to disparage 'Janeite' readers who like to hear in Austen's novels the companionable voice of a friend, literary theorists can seem more than a little robotic when insisting on impersonal language, not personal voice, as her narrative's defining characteristic. Pascal calls Austen's narrator 'he' because 'so truly is this impersonal narrator the "spirit of the story" that one cannot ascribe him/her a sex'. 'The narrator of *Emma* is not Jane Austen', an influential textbook by Mieke Bal reminds us, and so the book will 'here and there refer to the narrator as "it," however odd this may seem'.

Extreme versions of this position allow the presence of no narrator at all, just narrative as an autonomous discourse. And while there are good interpretative reasons for maintaining the author/narrator distinction as an analytic tool, to clamp it too rigidly on prose of such delicate fluidity is to risk sounding tone-deaf. These scholars don't of course resemble the early reader who responded to Austen's voice in *Pride and Prejudice* by declaring the novel 'much too clever to have been written by a woman'. But they underestimate the convergence between shaping author and narrating persona that Austen sometimes implies: a convergence, when one remembers the title pages of these novels (*Pride and Prejudice* is 'by the Author of "Sense and Sensibility"'; *Sense and Sensibility* is 'by a Lady'), that makes the gender reassignments of theory look somewhat obtuse.

Sometimes the narrating voice is a clarifying presence, and offers firm guidance in interpretation and judgement. The first chapter of *Pride and Prejudice* ends with a brisk but lucid character sketch of the ill-matched Bennet parents, and the analysis is later amplified with a careful blend of sympathy and severity that heralds the moralizing wisdom of Victorian fiction. Abruptly, one of the novel's running comic motifs—in which Austen has made us complicit by our laughter—is redefined as a real and many-sided ethical problem. We must understand the marriage in new terms, as a self-inflicted tragedy for Mr Bennet that has left 'all his views of domestic happiness . . . overthrown'. Yet while recognizing his predicament, and deploring the shallowness of his wife, we must also deplore, as dereliction of familial duty, the consolation he takes in mockery. Far from continuing to laugh with him, we must now condemn his 'continual breach of conjugal obligation . . . in exposing his wife to the contempt of her own children' (II.xix). Later still, Austen inserts a similarly rigorous analysis of the financial problem at the novel's heart, answering, with balanced fellow feeling and blame, essential but previously unasked questions about Mr Bennet's failure to defuse the ticking time-bomb of his entailed estate, which in time will leave his family disinherited—'for, of course, they were to have a son' (III.viii). Comparable moments of intrusive explanation elsewhere bring even the most unsympathetic characters within reach, if not of the narrator's compassion, then at least her understanding, including smarmy Collins and vicious Miss Bingley (I.xv, III.iii).

What makes moral analysis of this directness so arresting, however, is that it arises so infrequently, and as a rule also belatedly, after readers have first made their own judgements from conversation and action alone. In the comment to Cassandra, quoted above, about the scope for confusion arising from unattributed dialogue in *Pride and Prejudice*, Austen adds (riffing on a poem by Scott), 'I do not write for such dull Elves "As have not a great deal of Ingenuity themselves"'. The joke says much about her preference for coaxing readers, in the absence of full authorial explanation, to interpret and evaluate for themselves. Though willing

enough to give subtle, insightful assessments of her heroine's consciousness—'Elizabeth, agitated and confused,
rather *knew* that she was happy, than *felt* herself to be so'
(III.xvii)—Austen's narrator is pointedly non-omniscient
when it comes to Bingley or Darcy. Explanations of what
these characters think or feel are scarce, with emphasis
placed instead on the interpretative difficulties posed to
Elizabeth and Jane by their inscrutable acts or cryptic
words. In a novel preoccupied by uncertainties about true
character, by unreliable 'first impressions' and elusive
explanations, Austen's reticence—which extends to with-
holding key information, even active misdirection—
becomes a central technique, replicating Elizabeth's quan-
daries for readers, and involving us, like her, in efforts of
discovery. It's perhaps for this reason that Austen now plays
a starring role in the emerging field of literary neuroscience,
with experiments showing heightened patterns of neural
activity among subjects asked to read her fiction in
concentrated ways.

Free indirect discourse

Free indirect discourse—the illusion by which third-person
narrative comes to express, as though infiltrated by, or
emanating from, the intimate subjectivity of fictional
characters—was first conceptualized by Gustave Flaubert in
the 1850s. Austen has long been seen as the first major
exponent of this technique, so central to the modern
novel, for filtering narrative through the consciousness of
its subject, though few would now call her its inventor.

Sporadic instances of free indirect discourse—indirect because mediating a character's speech or thought via the narrator; free because able to roam from viewpoint to viewpoint—exist in Burney, Richardson, and earlier writers. Some linguisticians argue that deep structures of language make the style broadly available and apparently natural, with no one historical point of origin.

Yet before Austen, or after her until Flaubert and Henry James, it's hard to find any comparably sustained exploitation of free indirect discourse, and her novels beautifully illustrate the typical markers of the technique in both speech and thought. These include, fundamentally, an absence or suspension of reporting clauses (he said that/ she thought that), and the anomalous presence within third-person, past-tense narrative of linguistic features indicating a character's perspective and voice. Several of these features stand out: proximal deictics (now/here/tomorrow instead of then/there/the next day); backshifted exclamations ('How differently did every thing now appear in which he was concerned!' (II.xiii)); exclamatory questions ('What could be the meaning of it?' (I.xv)); unshifted modals ('She must own that she was tired of great houses' (II.xix)); syntactical informalities and fragments ('A few weeks, he believed' (III.xi)); character-specific locutions, especially inanities and vulgarisms ('how shocking it was to have a bad cold, and how excessively they disliked being ill' (I.viii)); 'it was much better worth looking at in the summer' (II.vi).

Free indirect discourse is at its most prominent in Austen's last novels, and its presence in *Northanger Abbey* probably indicates late revision. Even so, it's already a pervasive resource in *Pride and Prejudice*, most obviously as a way of catching in narrative prose the distinctive qualities of a character's speech, often for satirical effect. Consider the first visit to Longbourn of bloviating Mr Collins, which opens as detached, impersonal narration before shading into mocking ventriloquism (Box 4). Thanks to the preparation provided for this exquisite paragraph by Collins's preening introductory letter and Mr Bennet's amused response, it's easy to tune in to Collins's unctuous voice, and first to Mr Bennet himself, whose mischievous prompt can be reconstructed verbatim from the second sentence. Austen then shifts into narrative summary ('Mr. Collins was eloquent...') and reported speech ('he protested that...') before indicating the onset of Collins's effusion with an interruptive dash and two of his favourite terms for monstrous Lady Catherine—who, he elsewhere says, 'is all affability and condescension' (II.v).

From this point on the oleaginous wording, though rendered in the third person and backshifted in tense, is all Collins's own, as are the sentiments expressed. For of course there's nothing at all gracious about his patron or humble about his abode. These terms signify not reliable evaluation but Collins's self-deluding weakness for obsequy and cliché. Austen then gives him further rope to hang himself, not least in his gloriously unselfconscious confession about bunking off from parochial duty for weeks on end, a point that elicits a sarcasm from Elizabeth elsewhere (I.xiii). By the end of the paragraph, devoted in flatulent style ('vouchsafed') to pointless information ('shelves in the closets'),

---

BOX 4 *From* Pride and Prejudice, *I.xiv*

....

During dinner, Mr. Bennet scarcely spoke at all; but when the servants were withdrawn, he thought it time to have some conversation with his guest, and therefore started a subject in which he expected him to shine, by observing that he seemed very fortunate in his patroness. Lady Catherine de Bourgh's attention to his wishes, and consideration for his comfort, appeared very remarkable. Mr. Bennet could not have chosen better. Mr. Collins was eloquent in her praise. The subject elevated him to more than usual solemnity of manner, and with a most important aspect he protested that he had never in his life witnessed such behaviour in a person of rank—such affability and condescension, as he had himself experienced from Lady Catherine. She had been graciously pleased to approve of both the discourses, which he had already had the honour of preaching before her. She had also asked him twice to dine at Rosings, and had sent for him only the Saturday before, to make up her pool of quadrille in the evening. Lady Catherine was reckoned proud by many people he knew, but *he* had never seen any thing but affability in her. She had always spoken to him as she would to any other gentleman; she made not the smallest objection to his joining in the society of the neighbourhood, nor to his leaving his parish occasionally for a week or two, to visit his relations. She had even condescended to advise him to marry as soon as he could, provided he chose with discretion; and had once paid him a visit in his humble parsonage; where she had perfectly approved all the alterations he had been making, and had even vouchsafed to suggest some herself,—some shelves in the closets up stairs."

---

the text is saturated by his speaking voice—so much so that the first-edition compositor who typeset this paragraph closed it with a quotation mark (usually omitted in modern editions), though no quotation ever opens.

More intricate effects arise from Austen's use of free indirect thought, which, though developed in less sustained, psychologically probing ways than in *Emma* or *Persuasion*, is handled in *Pride and Prejudice* with greater mobility and range. Not only does the technique offer an intimacy of access to the heroine's consciousness that had never been so vividly achieved outside epistolary fiction. With startling flexibility, Austen extends the effect of telepathic insight to other characters, allowing readers to experience the novel's world kaleidoscopically as well as from within, and to look out by turns from multiple perspectives, albeit in fleeting ways, and with varying blind spots. In a narrative designed to reproduce for readers the uncertainties confronting Elizabeth and her sister, Darcy, Bingley, and Wickham are the marked exclusions. But even with enigmatic Darcy, Austen occasionally inflects the narrative with his voice, as when he recognizes, despite himself, Elizabeth's beautiful eyes and intelligent expression, and then her alluringly physical glow. It has been calculated that *Pride and Prejudice* filters its narrative, at different points, through no fewer than nineteen centres of consciousness, more than any other Austen novel (with *Mansfield Park*, at thirteen, the nearest competitor).

Yet categorical analysis of this kind can also be an illusion, for in Austen's hands the effect of free indirect thought is typically one of blending and blurring, not clear-cut counterpoint. By merging a character's idiolect with a narrator's syntax, by darting from viewpoint to viewpoint in adjacent sentences, and by studding passages of objective description with clause-length shards of free indirect discourse, Austen endlessly problematizes the origin and authority of her narrative statements. At the same time, she creates a remarkable narrative impression of conversational fluidity, often using rhythmic as opposed to strict grammatical punctuation to suggest the contours of consciousness in action or the informality of a speaking voice. Sometimes we sense a harmonious alignment of perspective between character and narrator, at others a more disruptive effect of irony or uncertainty. With this signature technique of her fiction, Austen calls on readers to navigate her prose with vigilance and discernment, and in a spirit that recognizes a lesson she would take further in *Emma*: that 'seldom, very seldom, does complete truth belong to any human disclosure' (III.xiii).

5

The Silence at Mansfield Park

At Cornell University in the 1950s, students of the novelist Vladimir Nabokov were assigned *Mansfield Park* each year before moving on to *Bleak House*, *Madame Bovary*, and eventually Proust and Joyce. Nabokov didn't think much of *Pride and Prejudice*, and chose *Mansfield Park* instead—'a comedy of manners and mischief, of smiles and sighs'—for its intricate plotting, formal perfection, and virtuoso precision of style. His lectures emphasize the work's thematic coherence, and the structural connections Austen creates between key episodes: episodes like the Sotherton outing and the *Lovers' Vows* rehearsal, both concerned with planning and scheming (parks, plays), the crossing of boundaries (material, moral), and the release of unsanctioned passions. Every aspect of the novel was exquisitely integrated and sequenced: 'Theme after theme opens its petals like a domestic rose.'

Mansfield Park now looks like a rather different work, or so the state of critical debate would suggest. Counter-intuitively, it has become a novel about offstage episodes and unspoken themes, global more than domestic. Nabokov didn't quite miss this global dimension, and he's among the first critics to have mentioned—with regard to the wealth of Sir Thomas Bertram, patriarch of Mansfield and also the owner of property in Antigua—that 'the plantations would have been worked by cheap slave labor, the source of the Bertram money'. But like other commentators of his era, he left the point undeveloped. It wasn't until Edward Said's *Culture and Imperialism* (1993), including a chapter on *Mansfield Park* and colonial sugar, that slavery came to dominate the critical agenda. For Said, here was a work of high aesthetic achievement and intellectual complexity, and 'the most explicit in its ideological and moral affirmations of Austen's novels'. Yet *Mansfield Park* was also a work with a glaring blind spot. While indicating the dependence of her characters on income from a contaminated source, Austen was unable or unwilling, or simply saw no need, to integrate the issue of slavery within the novel's overall moral scheme. The slave trade is mentioned, but just once, and then rapidly dropped.

Said's argument has influenced not only a wave of post-colonial readings—some nuanced and insightful, others piously blaming Austen for thoughtcrime—but also screen adaptations of *Mansfield Park*. In Patricia Rozema's film of 1999, new scenes and dialogue emphasize the plight of African slaves, and a slave ship is seen anchored off the English coast, where in practice it would certainly have been seized. (Slavery became illegal in England thanks to a common-law ruling of 1772, made, it so happens, by a judge named Lord Mansfield; the transatlantic slave trade was outlawed in 1807.) A dictatorial Sir Thomas Bertram, played with consummate menace by Harold Pinter, comes across in the movie as haunted by guilt, and finally sells off his Antigua estate.

In a letter to her sister Cassandra written just as *Pride and Prejudice* appeared in print, Austen said she was now trying 'to write of something else;—it shall be a complete change of subject—Ordination' (29 January 1813). Which means, at its narrowest, the admission of new clergy into holy orders or the established Anglican Church. Yet now it's as though Austen was writing—or, crucially, failing to write—about something else again: not the ordination of priests but the oppression of slaves. How might we understand this further change of subject, and can we connect what is said in *Mansfield Park* with what goes unsaid?

Authorship

We may certainly connect Austen's attention to the professions and professional life—not only the clergy but also the navy, represented in *Mansfield Park* by Fanny Price's adored, aspiring brother William—with her emerging self-image as a professional author. This self-image appears most obviously in her negotiations with publishers, conducted in concert with her banker brother Henry, and in her attitude to the novels as ways to secure income as well as recognition. *Sense and Sensibility* was published on commission (meaning Austen bore the risk but retained her copyright), and the sold-out first edition brought her £140. She then accepted £110 for the copyright of *Pride and Prejudice*: with hindsight an over-cautious decision, as her larger take from *Sense and Sensibility* makes clear. But at the time the deal allowed her to exult, roughly as she completed *Mansfield Park*: 'I have now therefore written myself into £250.—which only makes me long for more' (6 July 1813).

Mansfield Park certainly achieved that 'more', though we don't know the exact numbers. Most estimates suggest that the first edition of 1814, published on commission like *Sense and Sensibility*, brought Austen roughly £310, and perhaps as much as £350: nothing like the £2,100 achieved by Maria Edgeworth for her novel *Patronage* the same year, but heartening progress along the way. Alongside her increased earnings, this was also a moment of book-trade transition for Austen. Like its two precursors, *Mansfield Park* came out in the 'Military Library' of a midranking Whitehall bookseller named Thomas Egerton: at first sight an incongruous home for these novels, but a nice reminder that Austen was a wartime writer, alert to the pressures exerted on domestic life by global conflict, and to war as a source of instability and a driver of change (personal hazard, social disruption, professional advancement, romantic opportunity). Now, however, Austen's ambitions went beyond Egerton and his list. With *Mansfield Park* published and selling quite well (though for some reason it wasn't reviewed), she and Henry started talking to the prestigious publisher John Murray: 'a Rogue of course, but a civil one' (17 October 1815). After careful assessment, including advice from an influential literary journalist who praised 'your bankers sisters Novels' for their 'penetration and nature', Murray offered £450 for the copyright of *Emma*. He also wanted, into the bargain, the future rights to *Mansfield Park* and *Sense and Sensibility*.

Here Austen miscalculated again. She duly went ahead with Murray, but at her own financial risk, not his, refusing his offer to buy the copyrights. In the short term at least, these rights turned out to be worth less than she assumed, and indeed less than Murray (whose ledgers survive) assumed when calculating his offer. Printed in a run of 2,009 copies, *Emma* failed to sell out and had to be remaindered, while the second edition of *Mansfield Park*, a novel that perhaps by now had exhausted its audience, sold a meagre 162 copies in two years. When losses from the second edition of *Mansfield Park* (*c.*£182) were offset against profits from the first of *Emma* (*c.*£221), Austen received just £38 18*s* in total from her arrangements with roguish Murray.

The result is that her lifetime earnings as an author fall somewhere between £630 and £680, which by a widely used measure of relative purchasing power might mean £45,000 or £50,000 in modern money: not far short of the adequate £700 per annum that Edmund and Fanny will get from the living of Thornton Lacey in *Mansfield Park*, but again, this is Austen's total income for a six-year period, not an annual figure. In the long run these novels would of course make millions, but as John Maynard Keynes famously observed, in the long run we are all dead. In the short run, Austen salted her earnings away in 'Navy five per cents', a high-interest annuity issued by the Bank of England towards the end of the Napoleonic Wars, and the capital was still intact at the time of her death. But in 1816, a postwar economic slump led to the collapse of Henry's bank and put even wealthy Edward Knight under pressure. With financial support from her brothers under threat, the 'Profits of my Novels', as Austen calls them in a surviving manuscript account, were a matter of material importance as well as professional self-esteem.

Ordination

More significant for the purposes of reading *Mansfield Park* today is the commitment to seriousness of theme that accompanied Austen's growing sense of authorship as a professional vocation. This was the first novel she composed from scratch after a lengthy period of creative inactivity (in terms of composition if not revision) since giving up on 'The Watsons' in 1805. It's no longer the norm to make sharp distinctions between 'Steventon' and 'Chawton' phases of Austen's output—three novels first conceived in the later 1790s; three composed *ab initio* in the mid-1810s—but there's certainly a new artistic maturity about *Mansfield Park*, as well, perhaps, as a more recognizably conservative outlook on moral and social questions. As she contemplated moving on from her first publisher, Austen commented with regret that 'People are more ready to borrow & praise, than to buy' (30 November 1814), and she clearly aimed to move beyond the world of circulating libraries—the world of rapidly consumed, disposable fiction—and write durable books to be bought with rereading in view.

Her motivation went beyond mere sales, however. If artistic seriousness and commercial success were to come into conflict, her priority was always the former, even if that meant giving up the accessible, marketable pleasures of *Pride and Prejudice*. Just as Austen's fourth publication, *Emma*, was to run risks by featuring 'a heroine whom no one but myself will much like', so *Mansfield Park* sidelined amusement in ways that left her uneasy as she finished drafting the novel. To modern tastes, in fact, fastidious, virtue-signalling Fanny Price is a good deal less likeable than feisty Emma. But Austen was talking here about overall tone. 'I have something in hand—which I hope on the credit of P.&P. will sell well, tho' not half so entertaining', she wrote to her brother Frank, who like charismatic William Price was then on active Royal Navy service (6 July 1813).

It's worth adding that the same preference for instruction over entertainment is reflected in Austen's reading choices at this juncture. While composing *Mansfield Park*, the books she talks about are no longer circulating-library novels but serious treatises about public affairs. Notable among them is a widely discussed work of 1810 by Charles Pasley, a military engineer and strategic thinker, who emphasized Britain's over-reliance on naval supremacy and the real danger of annexation by Napoleonic France: the nation was 'menaced with destruction by a much superior force, which is directed by the energy of one of the greatest warriors that has appeared'. Pasley's *Essay on the Military Policy and Institutions of the British Empire* was written 'with extraordinary force & spirit', Austen told her sister. In fact, she playfully added, Pasley was 'the first soldier I ever sighed for', and she was 'as much in love with the Author as I ever was with Clarkson' (24 January 1813). Frustratingly, no letter survives to tell us more about her reading of Thomas Clarkson, the leading anti-slavery campaigner whose powerful *The History of the Rise, Progress, and Accomplishment of the Abolition of the Slave-Trade by the British Parliament* appeared in 1808.

To calibrate the distance of tone between *Pride and Prejudice* and *Mansfield Park*, we might contrast the treatment of self-command, a perennial Austen theme, in the two novels. The attitude is little changed, the method markedly so. It's a theme that generates a beautiful light-touch joke in *Pride and Prejudice*, when the new Mrs Collins, loyal but nauseated, seeks every means of getting her husband out of the house: on the subject of gardening, Elizabeth admires 'the command of countenance with which Charlotte talked of the healthfulness of the exercise, and owned she encouraged it as much as possible' (II.v). In *Mansfield Park*, by contrast, the same theme emerges not satirically but in a mode of sonorous truth-telling that recalls Samuel Johnson, the great 18th-century moralist, with his voice of discriminating wisdom and stylistic balance. At Sotherton, selfish Julia Bertram suddenly finds herself trapped in a subordinate role:

> The politeness which she had been brought up to practise as a duty, made it impossible for her to escape; while the want of that higher species of self-command, that just consideration of others, that knowledge of her own heart, that principle of right which had not formed any essential part of her education, made her miserable under it. (I.ix)

Mansfield Park is still intermittently very funny—those end-less reports, exquisitely timed, of HMS *Thrush* leaving Portsmouth harbour—but comedy now enters the service of edification. Like *Northanger Abbey*, *Mansfield Park* ends with witty gestures of authorial artifice and pragmatism (we may decide for ourselves how long it takes Edmund to switch his affections to Fanny), but also with a solemnly Johnsonian dictum about life as a condition 'of being born to struggle and endure' (III.xvii).

More broadly, we might contrast the satirical fun Austen has with the clergy in *Pride and Prejudice*—unctuous, toadying Mr Collins again—with the role allotted to Edmund Bertram as a model of civic virtue in *Mansfield Park*. Comic derision of timeserving worldliness now gives way, with Edmund as mouthpiece, to earnest disquisitions about a clergyman's vocation and the social and spiritual import-ance of ministry. In *Pride and Prejudice*, Collins's view of his duties as annoying distractions from self-advancement is scandalous but amusing, leaving Elizabeth struck by 'his kind intention of christening, marrying, and burying his parishioners whenever it were required' (I.xiii). With Edmund, however, Austen switches from negative satire into positive endorsement. There's no room to doubt her investment in his idea of parish work as central to the clergy-man's calling, and as the best guarantor of order, social and moral, in the nation at large. More even than the other professions (lawyer, soldier, sailor), the clergyman has 'charge of all that is of the first importance to mankind, individually or collectively considered, temporally and eternally . . . the guardianship of religion and morals, and consequently of the manners which result from their influence' (I.ix).

In this context, it's sometimes argued that when Austen talked about 'Ordination' as the novel's theme, she used the word in a broad sense of ordering or rectifying—setting in order, setting to rights—that went beyond its technical meaning in the Anglican Church. More broadly, 'Ordination' encompasses the whole dynamic of the novel, with its disordered individuals, families, and estates; *Mansfield Park* thus becomes a novel about reforming a host of moral, spiritual, and social dislocations, with Edmund—the ethically serious, professionally committed clergyman in waiting—as the key agent of change. It's no coincidence that Edmund delivers his most important speeches about the clergyman's calling at Sotherton Court, an environment freighted by Austen with a symbolism of boundaries and transgressions—fences, palisades, gates, ha-has—in the zone between unregulated wilderness and cultivated park (see Figure 6). By the end of the work, he and Fanny—a heroine whose goal is to experience life 'in a regular course of cheerful orderliness' (III.viii)—have emerged as leaders of a new generation that will reform the Mansfield estate and the community around it.

Slavery

When Edmund has said his piece about clerical duty during the Sotherton outing, 'a general silence succeeded' (I.ix). Nobody wants to talk, and after a pause the subject changes. It's not the first or last such moment in *Mansfield Park*,

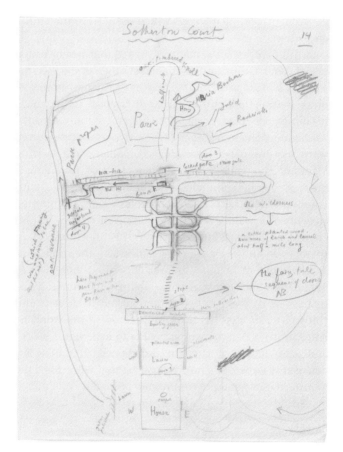

Figure 6 Vladimir Nabokov's map of Sotherton Court (c.1950), sketched in preparation for his Cornell University lectures on *Mansfield Park*.

which is not only a novel of smiles and sighs, but also a novel of silences: silences of different kinds that Austen specifies with care—determined, gloomy, indignant, luxurious, thoughtful. Early on, Fanny's benefactors at Mansfield—even kindly, lazy Lady Bertram—give her the silent treatment, or make her fall silent herself; Edmund gets silenced by the impropriety of Mary Crawford, and when finally forced to give her up, 'it was with agonies, which did not admit of speech' (III.xvi); Maria and Julia Bertram are silenced by frustration or pique, Sir Thomas by dismay or anger, his wife by stupidity or inertia, the Crawfords by their tactics and schemes. Only garrulous, bossy Mrs Norris seems immune to the silencing qualities of Mansfield Park, though at one point even she is 'a little confounded, and as nearly being silenced as ever she had been in her life' (II.ii).

Yet silence is never an absence of meaning in Austen's narrative, and it's often the reverse. It needs to be decoded, especially with Fanny, a character 'always more inclined to silence when feeling most strongly' (III.vi), and always inclined to interrogate it in others ('there were three different conclusions to be drawn from his silence', she thinks when Edmund sends her an elliptical letter (III.x)). Silence is everywhere something to probe, a mark of unconscious motive or repressed desire, or perhaps bad faith or secret design (Box 5).

So what should we make of the profoundest silence of all—the 'dead silence'—that follows Fanny's attempt, soon after Sir Thomas returns from his Antigua estate, to initiate a conversation about the slave trade. Is she simply being

> **BOX 5**   *From* Mansfield Park, *II.iii*
> ....
>
> 'Your uncle is disposed to be pleased with you in every respect;
> and I only wish you would talk to him more.—You are one of
> those who are too silent in the evening circle.'
>
> 'But I do talk to him more than I used. I am sure I do. Did not
> you hear me ask him about the slave trade last night?'
>
> 'I did—and was in hopes the question would be followed up
> by others. It would have pleased your uncle to be inquired of
> farther.'
>
> 'And I longed to do it—but there was such a dead silence!
> And while my cousins were sitting by without speaking a word,
> or seeming at all interested in the subject, I did not like—I
> thought it would appear as if I wanted to set myself off at
> their expense, by shewing a curiosity and pleasure in his infor-
> mation which he must wish his own daughters to feel.'

frozen out by her socially superior cousins, or is there something about the topic—as in *Northanger Abbey*, where 'from
politics, it was an easy step to silence' (I.xiv)—that leaves
those present unwilling or unable to speak? If so, what? Is it
simply boredom, on the part of Austen's bright young
things, with what had become a ubiquitous topic of public
debate in the years when the action is set? (*Mansfield Park*
gives out mixed messages, but Austen seems to have used a
calendar for 1808-9, which would put Sir Thomas in
Antigua in 1806-8, just as Parliament formally abolished the
slave trade.) Or is this a case of guilty conscience: an uneasy
recognition that the lifestyle the protagonists enjoy—'the
elegancies and luxuries of Mansfield Park' (III.vi)—depends,

largely or wholly, on suffering and oppression? These questions speak not only to critical debates about the Caribbean dimension of *Mansfield Park*, but also to the larger issue of Austen's approach to controversies of her time: fleeting, enigmatic and indirect, yet at the same time strangely pointed. Why bring the slave trade into the novel at all? And then why, having done so, leave the topic hanging without resolution?

This is not the only novel in which Austen raises the subject. It comes up by deft implication in *Northanger Abbey*, and in *Emma* with embarrassing directness; Austen may also have been planning to resume it in the fragmentary 'Sanditon', which brings in a young West Indian heiress, 'half-mulatto', presumably the daughter of a wealthy planter (ch. xi). In *Northanger Abbey*, no mention of slavery occurs when boorish John Thorpe transports Catherine, against her will, from Bath towards Blaise Castle, playground of a wealthy sugar merchant from the slave-trading port of Bristol (see Chapter 2). But the ironies in relation to Catherine's own situation are telling, the more so at a time when feminists like Mary Wollstonecraft were using Caribbean slavery as an analogy for the exploitation of women. 'Is one half of the human species, like the poor African slaves, to be subject to prejudices that brutalize them . . . ?', Wollstonecraft asked.

This is an analogy, of course, that might well be thought to trivialize the hideous situation of plantation slaves. But in *Emma*, Austen finds an ingenious way of accommodating the analogy while immunizing herself against the objection. Pressed with humiliating directness by Mrs Elton to seek employment as a governess, Jane Fairfax excoriates governess agencies as 'offices for the sale—not quite of human flesh—but of human intellect' (II.xvii). As so often, Austen reports the dialogue with little commentary, but Jane is clearly aiming a counter-thrust at Mrs Elton, whose family seem to have slave-trade connections, and who starts blustering about their abolitionist credentials. Jane then elaborates, repeating the governess–slave analogy even while denying that she makes it:

> 'I did not mean, I was not thinking of the slave-trade,' replied Jane; 'governess-trade, I assure you, was all that I had in view; widely different certainly as to the guilt of those who carry it on; but as to the greater misery of the victims, I do not know where it lies.'

Jane is conversationally on the ropes here, defending herself against faux-solicitous attack from Mrs Elton, and she understandably falls back on hyperbole. It's the perfect opportunity for Austen to plant in our minds the association between socially precarious women and chattel slaves without endorsing it in her own voice.

In *Mansfield Park* itself, Austen could certainly have been a good deal more explicit than she is about the subject her characters (except Fanny) don't want to discuss. In numerous small ways, the novel scatters quiet hints about slavery, and perhaps even does so with its proper nouns. Some readers find a nod to the Mansfield ruling of 1772 (outlawing slavery in England) in the novel's title; others find in the name of Sir Thomas's domineering sister-in-law, Mrs Norris, the echo of a prominent but troubling figure from Clarkson's *History*, a backslider from the abolitionist movement named John Norris. More explicit are the peri-odic reminders Austen gives about Sir Thomas's Antigua estate and the business problems there that cause him to undertake his voyage: 'recent losses', 'poor returns' (I.iii).

Like many of her readers, Austen no doubt knew about the French naval blockade (1803–7) of Britain's sugar-producing colonies, which disrupted shipping and drove several Antigua plantations into failure. Like the fictional William Price, both of Austen's Royal Navy brothers served in the West Indies at around this time, and Frank, aboard HMS *Canopus*, is known to have spent time in Antigua in 1805. He saw enough to form decided opinions about Caribbean slavery, and on voyaging to St Helena in 1808, he deplored the survival of slavery there while noting that it was not practised with the same 'harshness and despotism which has been so justly attributed to the conduct of the Land-holders, or their managers in the West India Islands'. Few of the letters now survive, but we know that Austen corres-ponded regularly with both brothers throughout their Royal Navy service, which after 1807 included enforcement of the new prohibition on slave-trade shipping in the waters between the West Indies and the southern United States. Frank came to embrace a radical vision in which slavery, as opposed to merely the trade, would be abolished in all the colonies (a reform finally enacted in 1833), and Britain would uphold 'the inalienable rights of all the nations, of what colour so ever they may be'.

Yet implication, not explication, was Austen's way, and though she obviously knew a great deal about slavery her-self, she adds little to supplement the novel's hints with clear interpretative guidance. Sir Thomas remains a conundrum throughout *Mansfield Park*, typically forbidding but occasionally benign (he's even credited at the end with 'charitable kindness' (III.xvii)). We never learn where he stands on the politically pressing issue of slave-trade abolition. He's a Member of Parliament, but we're given no information, pro or con, about the use to which he puts his voice and vote. Austen could perfectly well have positioned him as a self-serving anti-abolitionist, or she could have made him a reformist like the hero of Mary Brunton's *Discipline* (1815), a West India merchant who nonetheless excoriates the slave trade in Parliament, and zealously opposes 'this vilest traffic that ever degraded the name and character of man'. However, the kind of digression in which Brunton then indulges—'Alas! that a more lasting page than mine must record, that the cry of the oppressed often came up before British senates, ere they would deign to hear!'—was emphatically not her style. Her method was instead to present readers with puzzles and problems, and require them to exert their moral and intellectual faculties in thinking the problems through. As she said of *Pride and Prejudice*, her novels were for readers possessing 'Ingenuity themselves', and willing to apply it as they read (see Chapter 4).

The failed conversation about the slave trade, and the 'dead silence' that ensues, is at one level an activation of this process: an interpretative challenge to us to consider the disorders or ailments of Sir Thomas's two estates, in Antigua and at Mansfield Park, and the relationship between them. Yet it's also a telling observation about the failure of the beneficiaries of slavery—the goodtime girls and boys of

Mansfield Park, with their flirty amateur theatricals and parties of pleasure—to face up to the suffering that funds their leisure. Austen took her cue here from Laurence Sterne's *A Sentimental Journey* (1768), in which the well-meaning protagonist Yorick is prompted by the sight of a caged starling—'I can't get out, I can't get out—said the starling'—to think about Caribbean slavery. But Yorick then fails to make the necessary imaginative effort, and his thoughts collapse into self-indulgence and solipsism. Resolving to consider 'the millions of my fellow-creatures born to no inheritance but slavery', he then feebly finds, 'however affecting the picture was, that I could not bring it near me', and instead starts imagining a solitary prisoner in the Bastille. What makes the episode so devastatingly ironic is that Sterne was responding to a request from Ignatius Sancho, an African now living in freedom in London, to use his fiction to raise awareness of slavery and its evils. His solution was to identify, as the fundamental problem, the self-indulgence of sentimentalists who lacked the moral and imaginative energy to convert vague sympathy into philanthropic action.

On the Sotherton trip in the opening volume of *Mansfield Park*, frivolous Maria Bertram finds her enjoyment spoiled by the iron gate and other physical boundaries to the estate, which 'give me a feeling of restraint and hardship. I cannot get out, as the starling said' (I.x). Like Sterne's Yorick, of course she can; it's the slaves of her father's Antigua estate—the slaves she won't discuss on his English estate—who can't get out. The only character to think or talk about them is pious, moral Fanny Price, who, like her future husband Edmund, is firmly identified by Austen with low-church, evangelical Christianity (their overt religiosity in general; their disdain, more specifically, for fashion, theatricality, flirtation, luxury, and pleasure). The religious identity given to Fanny makes her a humourless killjoy, but it also associates her with the abolitionist campaign, which was powered above all by the evangelical movement, and makes her an appropriate agent for reforming decadent Mansfield Park in all its aspects.

Austen was overcoming an instinctive dislike of evangelical Christianity by the time she wrote *Mansfield Park*, and having declared 'I do not like the Evangelicals' when urged to read a didactic novel by Hannah More a few years earlier (24 January 1809), she was now 'by no means convinced that we ought not all to be Evangelicals' (18 November 1814). Her Sir Thomas does not, like Harold Pinter in Patricia Rozema's film, divest himself of his contaminated Antigua holdings at the end of *Mansfield Park*. But he is, she tells us, starting to grow 'sick of ambitious and mercenary connections' (III.xvii). With Edmund and Fanny installed in the parsonage and setting the tone, it's only a matter of time.

6

Emma and Englishness

In 1811 the future George IV—promiscuous, profligate, and an avid novel-reader—bought a copy of Jane Austen's first book, *Sense and Sensibility*, before the earliest newspaper ads had even appeared. She's unlikely to have celebrated, had she known. The Prince Regent's bulk order also included such titles as *Sicilian Mysteries*, *The Monk's Daughter*, and *The Capricious Mother*, and put her in fairly low-grade literary company. Moreover, Austen despised the Prince himself, figurehead of the kingdom and custodian of its welfare during the madness of George III, but widely seen as degenerate and delinquent. She took the side of the Prince's estranged wife in their embarrassingly public marital dispute, and with unusual vehemence: 'Poor Woman, I shall support her as long as I can, because she *is* a Woman, & because I hate her Husband' (16 February 1813).

As *Emma* went to press in 1815, Austen reacted coolly on being told by the Prince's librarian, James Stanier Clarke, that a dedication to his employer would be welcome. This was pretty much a command, and Austen complied. By the oleaginous standards of the day, however, the curt dedication she produced could hardly have looked more offhand. In twenty-nine frosty words, Austen drummingly emphasizes her dedicatee's rank ('HIS ROYAL HIGHNESS...HIS ROYAL HIGHNESS...HIS ROYAL HIGHNESS') but says nothing about the qualities or virtues that might, and should, underwrite it. In this of all novels, there's a withering irony to Austen's silence. *Emma* was her fullest exploration of the nation's moral health and social wellbeing, dedicated to the man charged with upholding these things, but pointedly failing to praise him for doing so. We must read the novel itself, the implication is, for better guidance.

Landscape

As *Emma* nears its excruciating climax on Box Hill—and what a feat to make a casual snub the fulcrum and culmination of a great novel—we encounter Austen's most concentrated evocation of the rural landscape (Box 6). English verdure, English culture (cultivation, agriculture), English comfort. The scene is sunlit but not scorched, muted and intimate yet tinged with majesty, bountiful and beautiful in complementary ways, messily unplanned yet somehow perfect. It's a pastoral idyll that magically conflates the seasons: autumnal smoke on a hot summer's day; spring blossom alongside ripened fruit. Realism is blissfully suspended in the interests of vision. Austen might almost be sketching directions for the cinematographers whose soft-focus renderings of the novels' settings are now central to the way we imagine her world.

Long before the first movie adaptations (*Pride and Prejudice*, 1940; *Emma*, 1948), the visual culture surrounding

BOX 6   *From* Emma, *III.vi*

It was hot; and after walking some time over the gardens in a scattered, dispersed way, scarcely any three together, they insensibly followed one another to the delicious shade of a broad short avenue of limes, which stretching beyond the garden at an equal distance from the river, seemed the finish of the pleasure grounds.—It led to nothing; nothing but a view at the end over a low stone wall with high pillars, which seemed intended, in their erection, to give the appearance of an approach to the house, which never had been there. Disputable, however, as might be the taste of such a termination, it was in itself a charming walk, and the view which closed it extremely pretty.—The considerable slope, at nearly the foot of which the Abbey stood, gradually acquired a steeper form beyond its grounds; and at half a mile distant was a bank of considerable abruptness and grandeur, well clothed with wood;—and at the bottom of this bank, favourably placed and sheltered, rose the Abbey-Mill Farm, with meadows in front, and the river making a close and handsome curve around it.

It was a sweet view—sweet to the eye and the mind. English verdure, English culture, English comfort, seen under a sun bright, without being oppressive.

In this walk Emma and Mr. Weston found all the others assembled; and towards this view she immediately perceived Mr. Knightley and Harriet distinct from the rest, quietly leading the way. Mr. Knightley and Harriet!—It was an odd tête-à-tête; but she was glad to see it.—There had been a time when he would have scorned her as a companion, and turned from her with little ceremony. Now they seemed in pleasant conversation. There had been a time also when Emma would have been sorry to see Harriet in a spot so favourable for the Abbey-Mill Farm; but now she feared it not. It might be safely viewed with all its appendages of prosperity and beauty, its rich pastures, spreading flocks, orchard in blossom, and light column of smoke ascending.

Austen, with its fantasy of rose-tinted Englishness, was deplored by her great successor Henry James. In Victorian editions and magazines, market-savvy publishers and illustrators found 'their "dear," our dear, everybody's dear, Jane ... so amenable to pretty reproduction'; Austen became the ultimate safe read, escapist, cosily nostalgic. Yet there's more to this very influential moment in *Emma* than heritage schmaltz, and the view looks forward as much as back, implying a vision of harmonious national renewal in a period of notable social instability and conflict.

Set-piece descriptions of landscape were never a big part of Austen's repertoire, and she had no interest, for example, in the noisily sublime descriptions of alps and storms that were a trademark feature of Ann Radcliffe's Gothic fiction. Instead, she emphasizes the picturesque, a category of taste that Henry Tilney discusses in *Northanger Abbey*, in which nature is arranged, with studied informality, as a source of affecting charm and pleasing freedom. Her landscape descriptions in this vein are always strategic, used in particular to indicate moral and aesthetic alignment. There's one such moment in *Pride and Prejudice*, when Elizabeth perceives Darcy's Pemberley estate as a place of organic harmony and spiritual refreshment, surveying 'the whole scene, the river, the trees scattered on its banks, and the winding of the valley ... with delight' (III.i). Yet Pemberley also conveys ethical meanings, to the point, on this occasion, of buying more uncritically into Tory ideology than Austen usually does. Its landscape expresses the Burkean values invested in Darcy as a benign exemplar of enlightened paternalism and responsible stewardship.

Similar idealization suffuses the Abbey Mill view, but this time with countervailing irony. A few paragraphs ahead of the verdure vision, gushy, self-absorbed Mrs Elton—English to the core, though in a far less appealing mode—slides from celebrating to disparaging strawberries, that nationally iconic fruit, in a passage of hilarious telegraphese:

> The best fruit in England—every body's favourite—always wholesome.—These the finest beds and finest sorts.— Delightful to gather for one's self— . . . inferior to cherries— currants more refreshing—only objection to gathering straw- berries the stooping—glaring sun—tired to death—could bear it no longer— (III.vi)

Englishness, the juxtaposition suggests, is not a single iden- tity but a contest of alternative possibilities: the brash ego- centrism of Mrs Elton; the ancient serenity she invades. Austen's own sympathies are unmistakable, and her loving evocation of Abbey Mill supports a broader project of cele- brating rural England and the society it nurtures. Yet the celebration brings with it a satirical flipside, and a keen sense, epitomized by predatory, materialist Mrs Elton, of trends that imperil the nation from within. In this respect *Emma* is, for all its apparent smallness of scale, a novel of large ambition. Beyond the intensity of its focus on charac- ter and consciousness (the consciousness, in particular, of a brilliant but frequently wrong-headed heroine), *Emma* is also a book about the state of the nation as it navigates the final dislocations of war and contemplates the fitness for the future of its social fabric.

Rank

Austen famously wrote that for a novelist, '3 or 4 Families in a Country Village is the very thing to work on' (9 September 1814). She sometimes disregarded the formula herself, but *Emma* stands out for its concentration on a single setting, a 'large and populous village almost amounting to a town' (I.i), and implicitly offers this setting as a microcosm of the nation. The narrative pinpoints its environment with unusual specificity—Highbury is 16 miles from London, 9 from Richmond, 7 from Box Hill—though the coordinates can't be triangulated on the ground. It's a small but busy community that is not yet suburbanized—as railways would make it in a Victorian novel—but is connected nonetheless with metropolitan life. The characters live among turnips, spring corn, and Alderney cows, but they can also get to London and back for a haircut or a picture frame. They have social and familial networks across the country—Bath, Oxford, Yorkshire; the fictional Maple Grove near Bristol—and take seaside vacations in Southend or upscale Weymouth. They're surrounded by regional products that demonstrate the national circulation of consumer goods: Stilton cheeses, Tunbridge-ware boxes, York tan gloves; a fancy Broadwood piano from Soho in London.

Then there are the people and the codes they live by. Centrally important throughout Austen's fiction are the structures, dynamics, and consequences of rank (a more useful term than 'class', with its Marxian baggage, for the intricate hierarchies of status and privilege at play in all the novels). It's in *Emma* that Austen unfolds the system in its finest and supplest calibrations, and she does so by refracting her narrative through the mind of a heroine firmly committed—unlike the more socially disruptive protagonists of other novels—to monitoring boundaries and keeping everyone in their place. She has a job on her hands, for *Emma* also registers the energies of social mobility in Regency England, but Austen's emphasis falls above all on the starting positions. With its distinct yet interconnected 'sets of people'—the phrase recurs in *Persuasion* and 'Sanditon', and in *Emma* accommodates 'the chosen and the best', the 'second set', and more (I.iii)—Highbury society connects, while also compartmentalizing, a broadly representative spectrum of genteel and middling-sort life.

This of course is not the entire social spectrum, merely its defining higher swathe. Modern readers are often struck by the marginalization of servants in Austen's fiction, though attitudes to servants are often freighted with meaning (it speaks volumes that Mr Woodhouse fusses about their welfare while Mrs Elton can't remember their names). If anything, however, it was the absence of aristocrats from *Emma* that struck early readers: that uppermost echelon whose lives Austen registers elsewhere (typically with derision) and were central to the genre of 'Silver Fork' fiction that became fashionable after her death. *Emma* lacked 'the highly-drawn characters in superior life which are so interesting in *Pride and Prejudice*', said the *Gentleman's Magazine*, but 'delineates with great accuracy the habits and the manners of a middle class of gentry; and of the inhabitants of a country village at one degree of rank and gentility beneath them'. When the novel came out in French in 1816, it was given the subtitle 'Les caractères anglais du siècle'.

At the apex of *Emma*'s world is Mr Knightley, the established country squire whose lands have been in his family since Tudor times. Near its foot are illegitimate but connected Harriet Smith and shabby-genteel Jane Fairfax; hanging on for dear life is penniless yet touchingly resilient Miss Bates, whose notice was once an honour, but no longer. Below them (in rank though not necessarily wealth) are the respectable bit-part players—figures like Mr Perry, Highbury's 'gentlemanlike' apothecary (I.ii)—who make up the social numbers when needed, and indicate the professional backbone of the nation's life. It's worth adding that patrician Knightley is sure enough of his standing to extend the spectrum further, preferring the company of his steward William Larkins and his tenant farmer Robert Martin to that of his fashionable neighbours.

Tellingly, Emma herself recoils from these indecorous contacts. She has no time for Knightley's unsettling idea, in Martin's case, of locating 'true gentility' in practical merit as opposed to technical rank (I.viii). She'll mingle with the well-born and minister to the poor, but 'the yeomanry'—rural freeholders, respectable farmers, and the like, too high for her charity, too low for her notice—'are precisely the order of people with whom I feel I can have nothing to do'. They're 'another set of beings', alien to her mind, though in fact playing a crucial role in making the world of Highbury cohere and thrive (I.iv). Throughout the novel, this anxious correctness of form identifies Emma's elite status as discernibly less secure than her future husband's.

Where Knightleys have owned land and lived from its yield since the dissolution of the monasteries (the name Donwell Abbey, like Northanger, is a reminder of ancient confiscation), the Woodhouses are relative newcomers to their 'notch' in the Donwell estate, and they live primarily from investments.

The same insecurity returns when the public dance proposed by Frank Churchill arouses Emma's alarm, not so much at the interpenetrations of rank involved in the dance itself, with its criss-cross of partners, but rather at the 'difficulty in every body's returning into their proper place the next morning' (II.vi). It's as though correct performance of social roles is itself a larger dance, strictly regulated, and not to be disrupted by casual interminglings. Equally alarming about this carnivalesque plan is the mindset it reveals in Frank himself, whose 'indifference to a confusion of rank, bordered too much on inelegance of mind' (II.vi).

In their relative lack of land and their reliance on capital, the Woodhouses lie close to the broad category of moneyed, professional, and rentier families—a category of non-landed affluence for which terms like 'new gentry', 'quasi-gentry', or 'pseudo-gentry' are sometimes used—who deferred to, emulated, and sought to enter the gentry proper. Often focusing their ambitions on the next generation, such families would emulate the lifestyle of the traditional elite, especially the outward trappings: elegant houses, spacious grounds, stables, and staff. They could buy or marry their way into circles above them, replenishing and energizing the old gentry while generating, in the process, local wrinkles or ruptures of social strata that were soon erased in some cases, enduringly visible in others. Beneath the serene surface of polite sociability, Austen frequently indicates powerful undercurrents of rivalry and conflict. The Woodhouses are as anxious to distinguish themselves from aspirational pseudo-gentry like the Eltons, or the wealthy, pretentious Sucklings at Maple Grove, as these families are to rise above the good-hearted but unpolished Coles—a parvenu family who, for all their wealth, have yet to acquire enough refinement to expunge the stigma of 'trade'.

In the civil but unrelenting competition for positional advantage that results, each participant displays the one-way vision that Emma attributes to Mr Elton, whose aversions and ambitions in courtship show him 'so well understanding the gradations of rank below him, and . . . so blind to what rose above' (I.xvi). When Elton marries money of uncertain provenance, his new wife—the absurdly named Augusta, with her even more risible sister Selina—is in Emma's eyes 'a little upstart, vulgar being' (II.xiv). But Mrs Elton expresses her own 'horror of upstarts' (II.xviii), and so the chain of upward aspiration and downward exclusion goes on. All subscribe to the hierarchy of rank in general while seeking to breach it in person. Yet full social acceptance proves harder to achieve than material wealth, and it's attained at best with the glacial pace of the Weston family, 'which for the last two or three generations had been rising into gentility and prosperity' (I.ii). In this, Austen's richest, subtlest analysis of England's social fabric and its principles of stratification, gentility and prosperity intertwine in intricate and keenly contested ways.

A national tale?

Emma differs profoundly, of course, from 'Condition of England' novels of the kind written by Austen's mid-19th-century successors—Gaskell, Dickens, and others—to address the urbanizing, industrializing present and the social problems arising. Austen casts only fleeting glances at the commercial powerhouses of the English regions: Mrs Elton's lucre is from Bristol, and so possibly the slave trade, though her rich brother-in-law, she claims, is an abolitionist; she sneers at arrivistes from Birmingham for 'expecting to be on a footing with the old established families' (II.xviii). London, which Austen knew and loved—'this Scene of Dissipation & vice...I begin already to find my Morals corrupted', she writes with glee during an early visit (23 August 1796)—is an offstage presence, but kept very firmly offstage. The capital's population was now more than a million, but the nation Austen inhabited remained largely rural, and *Emma* represents it that way.

Still less is this a 'National Tale' of the kind developed in Austen's lifetime by Scottish or Irish writers like Walter Scott and Maria Edgeworth, who drew on romance traditions to explore questions of culture and identity within a larger context of British nationhood. Austen is emphatically a novelist of England, not four-nations Britain, if only because writing from direct observation was her constant principle. 'Let the Portmans go to Ireland, but as you know nothing of the Manners there, you had better not go with them', she told her novel-writing niece Anna (18 August 1814)—so when Colonel Campbell in *Emma* takes his family to

Ireland, Austen leaves them to it. In an important review of *Emma*, Scott himself noted the fundamental differences of priority and practice between high-toned romances of Celtic identity and Austen's realist fictions of English life. Where Edgeworth used the grand sweep of the national tale, with scenes 'laid in higher life, varied by more romantic incident, and by her remarkable power of embodying and illustrating national character', Austen favours everyday occurrences, motives, and feelings, itemized with rigour and precision. Rereading *Pride and Prejudice* after her death, Scott added that while he himself could do 'the Big Bow-wow strain' of historical romance as well as anyone, he couldn't match her exquisite touch with the commonplace: 'That young lady had a talent for describing the involvement and feelings and characters of ordinary life which is to me the most wonderful I ever met with.'

This was higher praise than Austen got from Edgeworth, who couldn't see the point of Mr Woodhouse and his gruel, and gave up reading *Emma* after the first volume (of three). Yet it's precisely this everyday quality that makes *Emma* a national tale of its own alternative kind. For Austen's rejection of the genre's methods shouldn't be mistaken for rejection of its thematic ambitions; instead, she uses domestic realism to explore national identity as it exhibits itself, not across grand sweeps of history, but in a meticulously documented and nuanced here and now. The point is beautifully illustrated by another of Austen's exchanges with James Stanier Clarke—pompous, tone-deaf, and a glutton for epistolary punishment—shortly after he procured *Emma*'s dedication to the Prince Regent. She was now at work on

Persuasion, but he had a much better idea for her next project: the Prince's daughter was about to marry into the B-list German dynasty of Saxe-Coburg, so how about a romance based on the history of this august house? This was a proposal too far for Austen, who teasingly concurred (on April Fool's Day) 'that an Historical Romance...might be much more to the purpose of Profit or Popularity, than such pictures of domestic Life in Country Villages as I deal in'. However, she couldn't write such a thing to save her life: 'No—I must keep to my own style & go on in my own Way' (1 April 1816). As ever, she must write about what she knew, and what she knew was not German or any other national history but—with more acuteness than anyone living— English life in the present.

England in 1815

'England in 1819' is the title of a sonnet by Percy Shelley, posthumously published, which opens with a Lear-like vision of a moribund George III: 'An old, mad, blind, despised and dying King.' Written immediately after the Peterloo Massacre, when a mass meeting of industrial workers was violently extinguished in Manchester, Shelley's poem uses the king to symbolize corrupt authority and the dead hand of political oppression. This was two years after Austen's death, but Peterloo was only the culmination of a decade of economic dislocation and social unrest covering the entire period during which her novels appeared: a decade marked by poor harvests and food shortages, widespread unemployment, protests against agricultural and industrial mechanization (the term 'Luddism' originates at this time), and mass agitation for radical reform. Unrest was mishandled, and so exacerbated, by the clumsily repressive administration of Lord Liverpool, Prime Minister since the assassination of his predecessor in 1812.

Underlying these troubles were large structural changes, driven by the ascendant forces of commerce and finance, that disrupted existing patterns of social interdependence and empowered a newly acquisitive elite, unconstrained by paternalist traditions of responsibility and stewardship. Or so felt many former enthusiasts for the French Revolution, including Wordsworth and Coleridge, who by now had moved from youthful Jacobinism into a staunchly Burkean conservatism, but without losing their old radical animus against wealth and power dissevered from social obligation. Emphasizing the maintenance of harmony across ranks, Wordsworth deplored the erosion of communal bonds in an aggressive greed-is-good world of proto-capitalist self-interest. In a letter written soon after *Emma* appeared, he memorably expresses his fears of fragmentation and his sense of the causes (Box 7).

So what of England in 1815? There's nothing of this directness to be found in Austen's own correspondence, nor indeed her novels. This was a fiction of exploration, not polemic. She never caricatures the new gentry with the two-dimensional clarity of others at the time, and though she populates her world with monsters enough, she creates no one quite so rapacious as Sir Simon Steeltrap in Thomas Love Peacock's *Crotchet Castle* (1831), a landowner, magistrate, and scourge of the poor who shoots poachers and

BOX 7 *From William Wordsworth's letter to Daniel Stuart, 7 April 1817*

A Revolution will, I think, be staved off for the present, nor do I even apprehend that the disposition to rebellion may not without difficulty be suppressed, notwithstanding the embarrassments and heavy distresses of the times. Nevertheless I am like you, an alarmist, and for this reason, I see clearly that the principal ties which kept the different classes of society in a vital and harmonious dependence upon each other have, within these 30 years either been greatly impaired or wholly dissolved. Everything has been put up to market and sold for the highest price it would bring. Farmers used formerly to be attached to their Landlords, and labourers to their Farmers who employed them. All that kind of feeling has vanished—in like manner, the connexion between the trading and landed interests of country towns undergoes no modification whatsoever from personal feeling, whereas within my memory it was almost wholly governed by it. A country squire, or substantial yeoman, used formerly to resort to the same shops which his father had frequented before him, and nothing but a serious injury real or supposed would have appeared to him a justification for breaking up a connexion which was attended with substantial amity and interchanges of hospitality from generation to generation. All this moral cement is dissolved, habits and prejudices are broken and rooted up; nothing being substituted in their place but a quickened selfinterest, with more extensive views,—and wider dependencies,—but more lax in proportion as they are wider. The ministry will do well if they keep things quiet for the present, but if our present constitution in church and state is to last, it must rest as heretofore upon a moral basis; and they who govern the country must be something superior to mere financiers and political economists.

rackrents tenants, encloses commons and woodlands into his own grounds, shuts up footpaths and playing fields, and zealously punishes all property crimes. Austen knew as well as any satirist, however, that landscape is always political, and she reminds us of the fact when Henry Tilney's account of the picturesque in *Northanger Abbey* swerves suddenly into the question of land enclosure, and then into politics, from which 'it was an easy step to silence' (I.xiv). It's one of those eloquent silences in which Austen specializes, and alerts us to related hints about land and power throughout her work. On one side are the exploitative John Dashwoods of *Sense and Sensibility*, who dispossess the rural poor by enclosing (in other words, appropriating and privatizing) previously common grounds. On the other, there's benevolent Mr Darcy, of whom 'there is not one of his tenants or servants but what will give him a good name'. Elizabeth is entranced by Darcy's estate, but it's his sense of the duties of 'guardianship' conferred by his inheritance that seals the deal in her heart (*Pride and Prejudice*, III.i).

And then there's Mr Knightley in *Emma*, a grating figure for many readers today, but one who for all his faults—he's perhaps the most egregious mansplainer in any of the novels—embodies an authorial ideal. Austen's naming of characters in *Emma* is rarely innocent—the honest, upright Woodhouses; the parasitical Sucklings; the quasi-industrial Coles—but she's nowhere so emphatic as with chivalrous Mr Knightley and the good deeds he does at Donwell Abbey. He's as far as could be imagined from Peacock's Sir Simon Steeltrap, and he lives out the conscientious paternalism that Wordsworth feared was dying. Far from enclosing commons like Mr John Dashwood, he won't reroute the footpath to Langham for fear of inconveniencing local people. He walks when Emma thinks he should be seen in his carriage, and this carriage is of course just a functional thing, a world away from the four-wheeled bling—Selina's trophy 'barouche-landau' at Maple Grove—that Mrs Elton purrs endlessly about (II.xiv). He shops at Ford's like everyone else, not with the premeditation of Frank Churchill, who spends money there 'that I may prove myself to belong to . . . Highbury' (II.vi), but because he has nothing to prove. For the same reason, his rambling, irregular house is austerely unrenovated, with none of the modernizing opulence on show at Lady Catherine's Rosings or being planned at Sotherton by Mr Rushworth. Donwell is surrounded by ancient woods 'which neither fashion nor extravagance had rooted up'; it bespeaks 'true gentility, untainted in blood and understanding' (III.vi).

A key feature of this true gentility is a willingness to suspend distinctions of rank that more insecure members of Highbury's elite, like the arrogant, ambitious Eltons, police with such aggression. He thinks little of silly, illegitimate Harriet Smith, but when Harriet is publicly humiliated by Mr Elton, he makes a show of dancing with her; he pays scrupulous attention to tedious, downwardly mobile Miss Bates as an overt gesture of support. There's something almost egalitarian about his preference for the company of Robert Martin, his tenant but also avowedly his friend, over that of the Highbury elite. With this pointed selection of worth over birth, certainly worth over wealth, Knightley stands in contrast not only to the Eltons and their like but also to Emma herself, with her failure to recognize the 'yeomanry' as the backbone of England. In the courtship subplot concerning Robert Martin and Harriet, Austen is quite systematic in her play on the language of hierarchy—social or moral—as applied or misapplied by Knightley and Emma. For Emma, 'superior', 'inferior', and their cognates are terms of unyielding social distinction, so that Martin, undistinguished in birth and status, uncouth and unpolished in manners, is 'undoubtedly [Harriet's] inferior as to rank in society' (I.viii). Nothing else counts. But for Knightley, Martin's virtues—his probity, sincerity, and judgement; his fully earned prosperity—decisively trump his lack of breeding: he's 'as much her superior in sense as in situation' (I.viii).

It's tremendously important, in this context, that Austen's much-quoted evocation of 'English verdure, English culture, English comfort'—of a national identity grounded in landscape and the values it enshrines—is a view of Robert Martin's farm. If anything is idealized by this most playful and ironic of writers, it's the traditions and virtues associated with this worthy, unassuming farmer and the land he tends in a world of sneering Augusta Eltons and swanky barouche-landaus. We might even say that yeomanly Martin, and his bond of honest friendship with elite Knightley, is at the heart of Austen's vision of the national wellbeing: a wellbeing based on harmonious connections between social ranks, whose lives coexist and intertwine in mutually respectful, beneficial ways.

Austen, like Shakespeare, never ends a comedy without also striking a few off notes, and it's a notable feature of

Emma, even as marriages bring the protagonists auspiciously together, that broader social tensions are on the rise. When Harriet and Miss Bickerton are attacked and robbed by a gang of vagrants, the novelty of the event is the key point: 'Nothing of the sort had ever occurred before...no rencontre, no alarm of the kind' (III.iii). It's not the episode itself that makes Mr Woodhouse tremble and plead with Emma never to set out from Hartfield alone; it's the fact of new instability and disruption in the placid world he knows. Austen does not, as Wordsworth might, diagnose this small but alarming breakdown in the rural order with reference to new strains in the social compact, and she leaves us, as usual, to join the dots. But she also resumes the point in her final chapter, and we end the novel with a further reminder of rural dispossession and social unrest when, again to Mr Woodhouse's great alarm, thieves rob the local poultry-yards at night, an act of pilfering he fears will be a prelude to house-breaking. The mugging and thieving are fairly minor ruptures in the peace of Highbury, opportunities for jokes at Mr Woodhouse's expense, and episodes that Austen won't allow to contaminate her ending unduly. But she puts these disruptions there all the same, in conspicuous positions. A storm may be brewing on the horizon of the novel's tranquil landscape, she reminds us with her usual deft touch. England's moral cement is not quite dissolved, but it looks in need of careful, conscientious repair.

7

Passion and *Persuasion*

One reaction to the cult of Austen that developed in the Victorian era, and continues to flourish in the 21st century, was the allegation of bloodlessness. Here was a fiction minutely attuned to the intricacies of domestic life and the responses of individuals tasked with navigating complex, highly regulated social environments. But it was also a fiction unable to register psychological, or more specifically psychosexual, depth. The consciousness of an Austen heroine was always constrained or diminished by pressures of decorum; her inward life was never inward enough. For Charlotte Brontë, author of the emotionally expressive *Jane Eyre* (1847), Austen was unequalled in 'delineating the surface of the lives of genteel English people', but the passions were 'perfectly unknown to her'. She kept even the feelings at a cool distance. 'Her business is not half so much with the human heart as with the human eyes, mouth, hands and feet', Brontë wrote: 'what sees keenly, speaks aptly, moves flexibly, it suits her to study, but what throbs fast and full, though hidden, what the blood rushes through, what is the unseen seat of Life and the sentient target of death—*this* Miss Austen ignores.' Note that last twist of the knife: *Miss* Austen.

The same objection was made by American readers who associated the Austenolatry of their compatriots with a culturally suffocating Anglophilia: readers like Ralph Waldo Emerson ('Never was life so pinched and narrow') and Ezra Pound ('A book about a dull, stupid, hemmed-in sort of life, by a person who has lived it'). Yet a powerful counterargument also emerged, made by readers more willing to consider implication, and for whom Austen's most important effects were achieved obliquely. For Henry James, a pioneer of psychological realism in modern fiction, her heroines amounted instead to feeling in its purest form: 'a sort of simple undistracted concentrated feeling'. They did so in a mode, however, that required readers to probe below the polished surface of Austen's prose. The effect was most pronounced in the later works, for 'in of course an infinitely less explicit way, Emma Woodhouse and Anne Eliot [*sic*] give us as great an impression of "passion"...as the ladies of G[eorge] Sand and Balzac'. The passion was no less intense for being subterranean, for 'their small gentility and front parlour existence doesn't suppress it, but only modifies the outward form of it'. Here is a crucial insight for readers of Austen, and one illustrated with special force by *Persuasion*, a novel focused on the long, debilitating suppression of passion, and in the end its euphoric—also, its profoundly physical—resurgence.

Back stories

It's tempting to see *Persuasion* as the summation of Austen's oeuvre, though only the accident of untimely death makes it the last novel she completed. Perhaps in fact she didn't quite complete it, though the closing chapter—'Who can be in doubt of what followed?' (II.xii)—seems no more impatient than earlier novels in its last-lap sprint to the happy ending. *Persuasion*'s slightly unfinished quality is a matter of language, not plot. The novel's prose is often nervy and jagged, with less of the epigrammatic clarity that marks *Emma* or *Pride and Prejudice*, and it's to this feature that *Persuasion*'s air of passionate intensity is partly owing. The 'restless agitation' of the novel's characters (II.x) is reflected in its style, which is informal, even expressionist, to a degree not previously achieved by Austen. On 13 March 1817, shortly before illness made sustained writing impossible, Austen told Fanny Knight that *Persuasion* was now ready for publication and 'may perhaps appear about a twelvemonth hence', which suggests she had in mind her usual procedure of leaving a manuscript fallow for a while before entering final revisions. Had she lived beyond July, it's possible that *Persuasion* would have been given another coat of polish, and that the sketch-like immediacy of key passages would have yielded to high-gloss perfection.

Persuasion thus marks a terminal interruption, not a conscious conclusion, in Austen's creative life. Yet it also has, even so, the quality of a revisiting or recapitulation, perhaps in some respects a resolution, for author and protagonist alike (and it's hard not to suspect here—as Virginia Woolf, among others, suspected—that Anne Elliot is the heroine with whom Austen most personally identified). Memory is one of the work's central themes, and the pressures exerted by past choices—roads taken, roads not taken—on consciousness in the present, and on future life. As Deidre Lynch observes, the technical brilliance of *Persuasion* lies partly in the sense it conveys of being, not 'the typical "Austen novel"', but instead the sequel to such a thing: a novel we don't have in direct form, but one we're constantly reminded about, and prompted to reconstruct in our minds through a process of back-formation. Emotionally, intellectually, and simply in terms of her age, Anne Elliot is Austen's most mature heroine: a 27-year-old who has already lost her 'bloom' and 'glow' (key terms in the period's lexicon of sex appeal) in the wake of events that recall the Harriet Smith subplot in *Emma*. She doesn't, like Austen's earlier, younger heroines, enter afresh on the world of courtship. Instead, left on the shelf as the narrative opens, she plays ruefully out in her mind her self-denying refusal, years earlier, of the man she loved and continues to love. For Woolf, *Persuasion* proved, in its bleak articulations of regret, 'not merely the biographical fact that Jane Austen had loved, but the aesthetic fact that she was no longer afraid to say so'.

Expressively, there's something almost Tennysonian about this heroine's predicament for most of the narrative. She's immured in a festering emotional stasis that Austen registers in the dank autumnal environments around her: the 'small thick rain' that blots out the November landscape; the 'black, dripping, and comfortless' veranda at Uppercross (II.i). For Anne, this is an entirely conscious connection, an 'apt analogy of the declining year, with declining happiness' (I.x). Yet the forces that strand her in gloom and depression—a condition Austen names in this work (II.v) and evokes with delicate insight—are also those specified throughout the novels, from *Sense and Sensibility* onwards. Happiness is foreclosed, or so it seems for most of the narrative, by a toxic combination of social and economic pressures, exerted in this case by a meddling mentor for whom—in the novel's primal act of persuasion—Captain Wentworth is an ineligible marriage choice on grounds of both rank and income. *Persuasion* thus unfolds for the heroine as a clever but relentlessly painful reversal of the standard narrative trajectory of courtship fiction: 'She had been forced into prudence in her youth, she learned romance as she grew older' (I.iv).

Emma isn't the only prior story that *Persuasion* seems to revisit. In early 1816, Austen at last retrieved 'Susan' (the lost first version of *Northanger Abbey*) from the publisher who had bought but then spiked it, and over the next few months she seems to have been revising her old manuscript while also drafting the later episodes of *Persuasion*. There's no evidence that she foresaw their joint publication as *Northanger Abbey and Persuasion*, an event engineered after her death by Henry Austen. But she clearly thought of the two novels as having affinities, and links them explicitly in the letter to Fanny Knight quoted above (in which *Persuasion* is now 'ready for Publication' but *Northanger Abbey* 'upon the Shelve for the present'). Two things in particular connect the pair. With their shared setting—'it was all Bath', Anne thinks with dismay in *Persuasion*'s second volume (II.iii); the first volume of *Northanger Abbey* recounts 'a six weeks' residence in Bath' (I.ii)—these are Austen's most urban novels. A glamorous, opulent, but shark-infested social bubble, Bath in effect bookends *Northanger Abbey and Persuasion* as posthumously yoked in four volumes. It's an environment that gives free rein, as nowhere else, to Austen's interest in satirizing fashion, consumption, and predatory sociability in what in some respects—its World Heritage status now notwithstanding—was the Dubai or Las Vegas of her era.

Then there's the interest of both novels in reading, the psychological impact of reading, and above all the capacity of imaginative literature to equip or disable its most ardent readers for life in the real world. Here Austen intriguingly reverses the standard assumptions of her culture about gender and reading. *Northanger Abbey* was already unconventional in presenting a heroine whose immersion in Gothic fiction, though leading her to misjudge surface appearances, also helps her intuit the presence of something like Gothic oppression in modern guise: bullying John Thorpe; dowry-hunting General Tilney; the coercive social codes exploited by both. At first sight a familiar satire on female reading, the work is in fact more exploratory and double-edged. With grieving, self-absorbed Captain Benwick, however, Austen now presents a male reader whose obsession with the high Romanticism of Scott's poetry, and Byron's 'impassioned descriptions of hopeless agony' (I.xi), is almost entirely debilitating. By all the standard conventions of satires on reading, weepy broken-hearted Benwick should be a woman. Instead, he's a naval hero. In one of Austen's most exquisite touches, he's in fact the former lieutenant of the warship *Laconia*, a name connoting Spartan fortitude and resolve.

The irony is further enhanced when we read Benwick's conversation with Anne, who urges that 'it was the misfortune of poetry, to be seldom safely enjoyed by those who enjoyed it completely', alongside mirror episodes in *Northanger Abbey*. To discipline and contain Benwick's impassioned despair, Anne recommends exactly the kind of rational, moralizing, essayistic prose that Austen's narrator critiques in *Northanger Abbey* (I.v). Yet Anne makes this recommendation while also uneasily recognizing the resistance of her own deep passions to rational supervision. She becomes, as Austen puts it with a droll contrasting effect of stylistic control, 'eloquent on a point in which her own conduct would ill bear examination' (I.xi).

The navy

Other aspects of *Persuasion* indicate new directions, or at least a new approach to old themes. While resuming Austen's habitual analysis of society as stratified and ruled by time-honoured gradations of rank, *Persuasion* is frankly meritocratic in vision. Moves in this direction are already made in *Mansfield Park* and *Emma*, which valorize (beyond, or at least alongside, the traditional landed elite) the clerical profession and the non-elite 'yeomanry' respectively. But *Persuasion* takes the process a good deal further, and with sharper satirical bite. Preeningly immersed in his *Baronetage* and surrounded by dressing-room mirrors, Anne's father Sir Walter Elliot is an indolent narcissist, shallow and vain. At Bath, the much-anticipated 'Dowager Viscountess Dalrymple, and her daughter, the Honourable Miss Carteret', turn out on arrival to be 'nothing', mere ciphers with 'no superiority of manner, accomplishment, or understanding' (II.iv). It's not simply that inherited honours don't necessarily coincide with qualities worth honouring. True nobility now lies entirely elsewhere, and titles look like empty relics from a distant age. Mr Elliot, Sir Walter's reptilian heir, can still smoothly insist that 'rank is rank' (II.iv). But little more can now be said for a system that calcifies the social order in rigid, obsolete structures from the past, just at the moment when dynamism and renewal are most urgently needed.

Austen establishes the moment with unusual specificity, the 'present time' of *Persuasion* being, she tells us in her opening chapter, 'the summer of 1814'. The action unfolds, in other words, in the immediate past, during the phony peace between Napoleon's abdication and exile to Elba (April 1814) and the brief but alarming resumption of war that followed his escape a year later. Austen began drafting *Persuasion* the following August, by which time the final defeat of Napoleon at the Battle of Waterloo (June 1815) had greatly boosted the prestige of the British military—a point she jokily reflects in the unfinished 'Sanditon', where modish Mr Parker regrets naming his home Trafalgar House, 'for Waterloo is more the thing now' (ch. iv). For many, however, the all-important institution was still the Royal Navy, a body credited since the Revolutionary Wars of the 1790s with securing the nation, its colonies, and its lines of supply from numerous blockades and invasion scares. Among other peacetime roles, the navy now acted as a circum-Atlantic police force charged with intercepting slave-trading vessels.

There's no doubting Austen's participation in this national mood, in ways certainly reinforced by the example of her naval brothers. In *Persuasion*, Captain Wentworth and his fellow officers exhibit virtues arising from their profession—individual self-discipline, collective inter-reliance, entrepreneurial energy (from the 'prize money' system rewarding capture of enemy ships)—but also transferable to life ashore. The navy thus comes to offer a salutary model of national progress in the postwar future that now beckons. In the novel's remarkable closing endorsement—the last words Austen's contemporaries heard from her in print—the naval profession is also, 'if possible, more distinguished in its domestic virtues than in its national importance' (II.xii). But unalloyed celebration was never quite Austen's style, even in the atmosphere of residual trauma and patriotic hope that prevailed when the novel was written. With its strikingly worded reference to the 'tax of quick alarm' paid by naval families, Austen's closing sentence also carries a sting. The war her characters think is over will shortly erupt again—for as Milton famously asks in his sonnet to Fairfax, what can war but endless war still breed?

Captain Wentworth, now a notable hero and self-made man, embodies the naval virtues with distinction enough. But these virtues are enshrined most winningly of all in Admiral Croft, in all respects the antithesis of landlocked General Tilney in *Northanger Abbey*: genial, unpretentious, and conspicuously besotted (the feeling is mutual) by his gutsy seafaring wife. No couple in Austen is portrayed with greater affection than the inseparable Crofts, with their weather-beaten faces, their unfailing good nature, and their endearingly reckless driving. And while (as with the central concepts of *Sense and Sensibility*) it's never wise to think of Austen as a novelist who deals in polar opposites, the contrast between decadent Sir Walter and his energetic tenants, and the clashing social visions they represent, looks very pointed. Protected in wartime by Admiral Croft and his like, whose money saves him in peacetime from financial ruin, Sir Walter nonetheless disparages the navy for 'bringing persons of obscure birth into undue distinction, and raising men to honours which their fathers and grandfathers never dreamt of' (I.iii). A spokesman for rank-based immobility and social petrification, he scorns the novel's most exuberant representatives of life and love (though again Austen complicates her picture by making the Crofts, domestic paragons, also childless). It's for good reason that when Sir Walter at last vacates his ancestral estate, and the Crofts move in, Anne 'could not but in conscience feel that they were gone who deserved not to stay, and that Kellynch-hall had passed into better hands than its owners'' (II.i).

Even so, the naval heroes of *Persuasion* are not without their more ridiculous side. It's not simply that Captain Benwick, with his tough-minded service across the globe, can't read verses by Byron on 'dark blue seas' without getting all weepy (I.xii), or that Admiral Croft, veteran of Trafalgar, can't drive his gig on land without crashing into a dung-cart or flipping it over. For all their cool handling (we assume) of countless high-stakes emergencies at sea, none of Austen's masters and commanders seems able to cope when flighty, flirty Louisa Musgrove concusses herself in the novel's pivotal scene: her fall from an ancient harbour wall, the celebrated medieval Cobb at Lyme in Dorset. Theoretically, the nation's saviours should take this minor crisis in their stride. But as so often in Austen's art, fun trumps ideology and thematic pattern (Box 8).

It's a passage of great stylistic virtuosity, pitched beautifully between melodrama and farce, with sudden switches between elegant, measured narrative prose and the quick syntactic informality of a sketch. Some touches come close to Gothic excess: conjunction-free asyndeton ('no wound, no blood, no visible bruise'); cheesily inverted word order ('she breathed not'). Elsewhere, studiously crafted periodic sentences point up, by way of stylistic contrast, the failure of anyone on the scene to maintain their own balance. Louisa's sister gets in on the act by fainting too, while self-absorbed Mary not only fails to help but also immobilizes her husband, who otherwise might. The most spectacularly counter-productive reaction, however, is that of Captain Wentworth, hero of Santo Domingo, who, having failed to catch Louisa in the first place, now staggers around in agony and despair, imploring help for himself. Only Anne Elliot keeps a cool head, and realizes it might be an idea to send for a surgeon.

Oceanic Austen

Louisa's fall from the Cobb is the turning-point of Austen's plot, and the location she selects is rich in meaning. For Lyme was no tame, elegant resort like Brighton or Weymouth, but a place strongly marked by historical trauma, and celebrated for its natural wonders. A puritan

BOX 8   *From* Persuasion, *vol. 1, ch. 12*

There was too much wind to make the high part of the new Cobb pleasant for the ladies, and they agreed to get down the steps to the lower, and all were contented to pass quietly and carefully down the steep flight, excepting Louisa; she must be jumped down them by Captain Wentworth. In all their walks, he had had to jump her from the stiles; the sensation was delightful to her. The hardness of the pavement for her feet, made him less willing upon the present occasion; he did it, however; she was safely down, and instantly, to shew her enjoyment, ran up the steps to be jumped down again. He advised her against it, thought the jar too great; but no, he reasoned and talked in vain; she smiled and said, 'I am determined I will:' he put out his hands; she was too precipitate by half a second, she fell on the pavement on the Lower Cobb, and was taken up lifeless!

There was no wound, no blood, no visible bruise; but her eyes were closed, she breathed not, her face was like death.— The horror of the moment to all who stood around!

Captain Wentworth, who had caught her up, knelt with her in his arms, looking on her with a face as pallid as her own, in an agony of silence. 'She is dead! she is dead!' screamed Mary, catching hold of her husband, and contributing with his own horror to make him immoveable; and in another moment, Henrietta, sinking under the conviction, lost her senses too, and would have fallen on the steps, but for Captain Benwick and Anne, who caught and supported her between them.

'Is there no one to help me?' were the first words which burst from Captain Wentworth, in a tone of despair, and as if all his own strength were gone.

'Go to him, go to him,' cried Anne, 'for heaven's sake go to him. I can support her myself. Leave me, and go to him. Rub her hands, rub her temples; here are salts,—take them, take them.'

stronghold in the 17th century, Lyme survived royalist siege and bombardment in the Civil Wars, and in 1685 was the epicentre of the Duke of Monmouth's failed rebellion; following the notorious Bloody Assizes, local recruits to the rising were hanged on the beach. Now, heavy landslips and coastal erosions were exposing distant reaches of geological time of exactly the kind, a generation later, that would so unsettle Victorian authors like the Tennyson of *In Memoriam*. The self-taught palaeontologist Mary Anning was just a child when Austen stayed in Lyme and mentioned Anning's father in a letter (14 September 1804). But by the time of *Persuasion* her sensational finds in the local strata—most famously, a complete ichthyosaur skeleton in 1812—were widely publicized, though their full implications were not yet grasped.

None of these associations explicitly enters Austen's text, but they give rich underlying resonance to her description of Lyme: a resonance sensed by Tennyson himself, who decades later was moved to go there 'by the description of the place in Miss Austen's *Persuasion*'. It's certainly a memorable description. Austen was in general suspicious of the oceanic sublime (in 'Sanditon', Sir Edward hilariously mangles the mode 'in a tone of great Taste and Feeling', ch. vii) but in *Persuasion* she evokes Lyme's dramatic coastline, today branded 'the Jurassic Coast', with special eloquence. Like her exact contemporary J. M. W. Turner, whose sketches and paintings render Lyme Bay with a visionary intensity that transcends descriptive realism (see Figure 7), she reaches here for an almost otherworldly effect. Lyme becomes a place of ancient mystery and preternatural depth, radically apart from the superficial social environments

Figure 7 J. M. W. Turner, *Lyme Regis* (*c*.1834), Cincinnati Art Museum. *Lyme Bay fascinated Turner for decades; a comparable watercolour of c.1812 is now at Kelvingrove Art Gallery, Glasgow.*

from which the characters have travelled, and to which they'll return.

Most exotic of all is the violently eroded undercliff west of the town, 'with its green chasms between romantic rocks, where the scattered forest trees and orchards of luxuriant growth declare that many a generation must have passed away since the first partial falling of the cliff prepared the ground for such a state, where a scene so wonderful and so lovely is exhibited' (I.xi). It's an environment closer to the tumultuous Dorset of a Thomas Hardy novel than to decorous Kellynch or glitzy Bath. Not coincidentally, it's also an environment in which Austen's heroine at last becomes fully alive, her inner depths no longer held back by the enduring depression—the 'great tendency to lowness' (I.xi)—of her years since rejecting Wentworth.

For the critic Peter W. Graham, this very specific coastal setting prepares Anne 'to turn her back on those dying dinosaurs among whom she's lived, the landed Elliots, and to cast her lot with the ascendant meritocracy of the British navy, the captains whose ships rule the waves where plesiosaurs and ichthyosaurs once swam'. Austen may not have planned *Persuasion* with quite such programmatic neatness, and if she connected the crumbling strata and ancient monsters of Lyme with the rank-based fossilization of Regency society, it's a connection she leaves the reader to disinter. There's no question, however, that she uses the inherent romanticism of Lyme to express something fundamental, and fundamentally passionate, about the heroine of *Persuasion*. Indeed, the place not only expresses Anne's deepest nature by association, but also literally revives her, and brings her long-buried passions back to the surface. In the seaside interlude of *Mansfield Park*, Austen shows Fanny Price in prissy recoil from the mess, noise, and indecorum, but also the compelling energy and vigour, of her Portsmouth kin. At Lyme, Anne Elliot does exactly the reverse, and with raw, implicitly sexual, physicality: with 'the bloom and freshness of youth restored by the fine wind . . . blowing on her complexion' (I.xii). No longer haggard with regret and self-denial, she starts catching roving eyes, and surprises her former lover into rekindled desire.

From this perspective, the first volume of *Persuasion* narrates not a shallow capacity for passion but the crushing psychological consequence of wrong decisions and ongoing regret. Austen itemizes the symptoms with unsparing directness: 'certain immediate wretchedness' (I.iv); 'a sort of desolate tranquillity' (I.v); 'silent, deep mortification' (I.vii), 'a confusion of varying, but very painful agitation' (I.ix); a plangent sense of blight as total and irremediable, when 'eight years, almost eight years had passed, since all had been given up' (I.vii). And while Brontë is absolutely right to note Austen's meticulous attention to the hands and the eyes, she fails to add that these, too, become registers of the mind and the heart. When Anne dutifully plays the piano so that others can dance, her eyes fill with tears as her hands touch the keys, but nobody seems to notice (I.viii).

None of this would mean a great deal if merely reported from the outside. But in comparison with the diffused narrative perspectives of *Pride and Prejudice*, or the ironic effects arising from *Emma*'s frequent misperceptions of people around her, *Persuasion* achieves an unprecedented intensity of focus on the consciousness of its heroine. With this focus comes a newly powerful illusion of penetration and depth, not only in Anne's abiding sorrow, but also in her exuberant regeneration, her emergence into 'joy, senseless joy!' (II.vi). Indeed, it's her long-ingrained performance of calm that gives this eventual revival its special force, 'smiles reined in and spirits dancing in private rapture' (II.xi). It's a revival moreover, that Austen presents (to return to the terms of Brontë's objection) as also overwhelmingly a matter of the pulse and the body, of blood and what the blood runs through. In counterpoint with the sterile 'baronet-blood' of Sir Walter or the designs of 'cold-blooded' Mr Elliot, Anne's overspreading blushes and recolouring bloom in the second volume of *Persuasion*, like the 'eyes of glowing entreaty' that Wentworth returns her, mark her liberation as a corporeal fact (I.i; II.ix; II.xi).

It's a euphoric conclusion, and also, in its joyful transcendence of inherited authority and social convention, a markedly transgressive one. That may be why the first published review of *Northanger Abbey and Persuasion*, in the *British Critic* for March 1818, devoted eight pages to the former novel and just three disapproving sentences to the latter. *Persuasion* was clearly the work of the same mind as *Northanger Abbey*, and had passages of outstanding merit, the reviewer acknowledged. But it also conveyed a deplorable message, that passion should trump prudence in courtship and marriage. In fact, *Northanger Abbey* itself waves a red rag to critics by playfully wondering, in the final sentence, whether its plot ends up rewarding disobedience and rebellion. Now, the final chapter of *Persuasion* more openly admits, 'this may be bad morality to conclude with' (II.xii). Bad morality, but also truth to life. Creatively, and in relation to the stifling expectations of decorum and didacticism that still constrained published fiction, the liberation won in *Persuasion* was also Austen's own.

Afterword

Jane Austen died on 18 July 1817, days after composing a jauntily anapaestic poem on the Winchester races, with its jokes about untimely rain on St Swithun's Day. Her last known letter is deeply moving—a loving tribute to Cassandra, 'my dearest sister, my tender, watchful, indefatigable nurse'—but then moves into a sly comic turn concerning poor deportment and fat legs. As she writes with the waspish economy of the published novels, 'You will find Captain —— a very respectable, well-meaning man, without much manner, his wife and sister all good humour and obligingness, and I hope (since the fashion allows it) with rather longer petticoats than last year' (29 May 1817).

With four of the six novels now in print, Austen's reputation was on the rise when she died, though not yet high enough for her burial in Winchester Cathedral (a rare honour) to be explained except as the result of strings being pulled by family members. One of them, Henry Austen, wrote a short biography that was published the following December with *Northanger Abbey and Persuasion*; later memoirs by other relatives lamented the curtailment of her creative life just as it bloomed into full maturity. It was left, much later, to Austen's most brilliant reader of the modernist era, Virginia Woolf, to look counterfactually forward to a future that had been cut off: to the thought of 'Jane Austen at Sixty', in the title affixed to Woolf's review of R. W. Chapman's 1923 edition of the novels.

For Woolf, *Persuasion* was the work of a writer manifestly on the cusp of creative transformation, tiring of her tried and tested routines, displaying an altered attitude to life, and poised to write in exciting new ways. In part, what Woolf imagines is an evolution of technique, an intensifying emphasis on consciousness over conversation—'this is already perceptible in *Persuasion*'—as Austen's central means of revealing character. In part, Woolf imagines a more worldly Austen, lionized in London, hobnobbing with the great, whose existing methods 'would have become too crude to hold all that she now perceived of the complexity of human nature'. Above all, she imagines a change of tone: 'Her satire, while it played less incessantly, would have been more stringent and severe.'

All this is speculation, of course, and the interest of Woolf's essay lies partly in its element of self-projection, as though what really drives her analysis is a vision of Austen morphing into Woolf herself, or at least a prediction of Woolf. That said, it's hard to read the twelve bravura chapters of the unfinished 'Sanditon', dashed off as Austen's health declined in the first two to three months of 1817 (we have perhaps 20 per cent of a full-length novel), without a sense of an author striking boldly out in fresh directions. To be sure, the work shows numerous thematic continuities with the existing novels, notably in Austen's perennial concern with courtship and the complicating obstacles of rank and wealth. Visiting pupils from a London ladies' seminary, 'very accomplished and very Ignorant', allow her to pick up the Wollstonecraftian satire on female education that lurks within other novels, 'the object of all . . . to captivate some Man of much better fortune than their own' (ch. xi). Austen was probably still reworking *Northanger Abbey* when she started on 'Sanditon', and she resumes that novel's self-consciousness about circulating libraries and the fiction that filled them, notably in the character of Sir Edward Denham, a single-minded but incompetent rake who 'had read more sentimental Novels than agreed with him' (ch. viii).

As for the question of style and technique, some of the most marked differences between 'Sanditon' and the published novels must be attributed to their different textual states, 'Sanditon' being unfinished in a dual sense, its plot incomplete but also its prose unrevised (though Austen is constantly sharpening wording as she composes). The surviving manuscript is a working draft, brisk, unparagraphed, and punctuated by dashes, and the energy it communicates has much to do with the glimpse it allows of the creative moment, without the high polish of later reflection (see Figure 8). It was Austen's practice to set aside a completed draft for several months before revising with fresh eyes, and 'Sanditon' would have been no different.

Other emphases are very new. The work-in-progress was known in the family as 'The Brothers', but the published title of 1871 has stuck. It perfectly catches Austen's focus on place, and also, in literal and metaphorical senses, the arenaceous instability of the place. For the fictional Sanditon, a

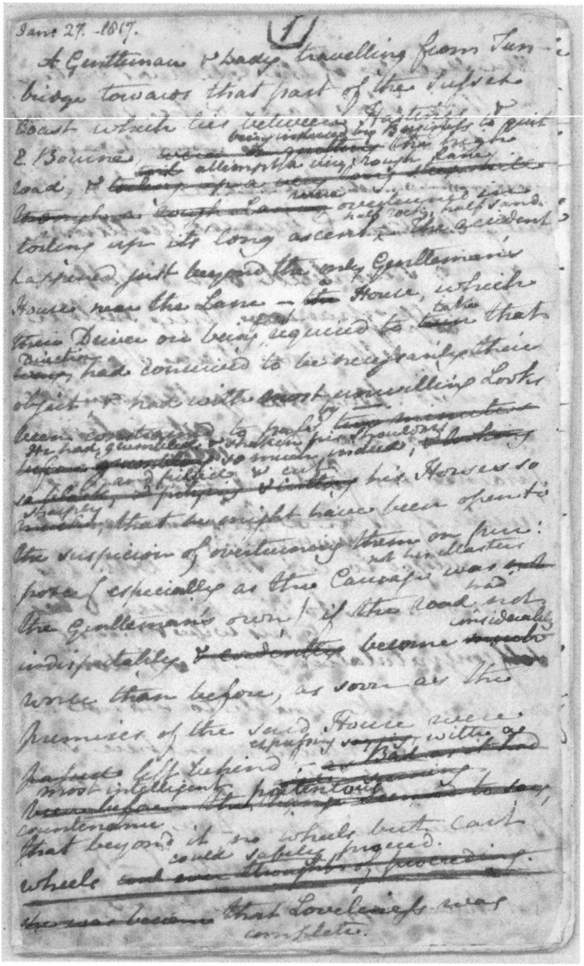

Figure 8 The densely overwritten opening page of the 'Sanditon' holograph, which Austen began in January 1817 and abandoned in March, four months before her death.

fishing village now being developed by speculators as a health resort, becomes in Austen's hands the focus of modern commercial energies of kinds that had previously lurked in the background of her fiction, but had never really stepped to the fore. 'Speculation' is one of the key words in this narrative about projectors building on sand: 'bad Speculation', 'profitable Speculation', 'his Mine, his Lottery, his Speculation' (chs i, ii). 'Business' is another key term, as Austen announces when nuancing a phrase in her opening sentence, originally 'quitting the high road', to read, more tellingly, 'being induced by Business to quit the high road' (ch. i). This is a work in which real-estate development and medical consumerism meet Austen's long-standing interest in transactional marriage. It's also a work populated by characters who look forward to the comedy of entrepreneurship in Victorian fiction. 'Never was there a place more palpably designed by Nature for the resort of the Invalid—', declares Mr Parker with an almost Dickensian exuberance: 'the very Spot which Thousands seemed in need of.—The most desirable distance from London!' (ch. i).

How Austen would have gone on to intertwine these themes can never be known, but the new scope or ambition is clear enough, alongside her ongoing interest in socioeconomic contrasts and tensions within the broad elite. Wealthy, sickly Miss Lambe, 'about seventeen, half-mulatto, chilly and tender' (ch. xi), is the first brown person in Austen's fiction. And though she enters the manuscript only for its last four chapters, Miss Lambe appears to be being lined up by Austen for a courtship subplot involving Sir Edward, a foolish baronet vaingloriously obsessed with lineage and ancient prestige: a young Sir Walter Elliot, in effect. If so, Austen was on the brink of engineering the boldest of her many fictional misalliances.

In the end, Jane Austen at 60—Austen on the cusp of the Victorian era, and in Woolf's eyes 'the forerunner of Henry James and of Proust'—is a phenomenon too rich to be fully imagined. But from Jane Austen at 40 we have quite enough achievement to be going on with. Technically, with the eloquent economy of her satirical insinuations and psychological hints, she was a pioneer of the novel genre whose impact—if impact is the word for a writer of such transcendent subtlety—continues to be felt. Thematically, she probed what her era called the recesses of the heart and mind, while also exploring, with astonishing penetration, the consequences for heart and mind of overarching circumstances, structures, and interactions. With her characteristic blend of delicacy and defiance, she told the Prince Regent, via his librarian, that as a novelist she must keep to her own style of fiction, and 'go on in [her] own Way' (1 April 1816). Millions of us have followed her down it ever since, gaining something like the view caught by her sister in a beautiful, teasing watercolour sketch of 1804 (see Figure 9). Considered as a portrait, it's the kind of image we might more readily associate with modernist inscrutability, as in Cecil Beaton's celebrated 1941 photoshoot of Henry Green, focused with exquisite care on the novelist's back. Yet the sketch also catches something important about Austen, her narrative style, and the authorial stance she adopts: poised yet also informal, even intimate to some degree, but with no interest at all in showing her face.

Figure 9 Watercolour sketch of Jane Austen by her sister Cassandra, signed C.E.A. and dated 1804.

TIMELINE

Note: Some dates of composition are conjectural.

1775   Born in Steventon, Hants, on 16 December

1783   Tutored in Oxford and Southampton with sister Cassandra

1785–6   Attends the Abbey House School in Reading with Cassandra

1787–93   Writes three volumes of manuscript juvenilia for family entertainment

1788   Visits London for the first time

1794   Writes 'Lady Susan'

1795   Writes 'Elinor & Marianne' (first draft of *Sense and Sensibility*)

1796   Courted by Tom Lefroy; starts writing 'First Impressions' (first draft of *Pride and Prejudice*)

1797   Death of Cassandra's fiancé Tom Fowle; completes 'First Impressions', which is offered to, and rejected by, publisher Thomas Cadell; starts recasting 'Elinor & Marianne' as *Sense and Sensibility*; visits Bath for the first time

1798–9   Writes 'Susan' (first draft of *Northanger Abbey*)

1801   Moves with family to Bath, making seasonal visits to Lyme and other seaside resorts over the next few years

1802	Accepts, and the next day rejects, marriage proposal from Harris Bigg-Wither; revises 'Susan'
1803	Sells 'Susan' for £10 to Benjamin Crosby, who advertises it but fails to publish
1804	Starts writing 'The Watsons'
1805	Death of father George Austen; abandons 'The Watsons'
1806	Settles in Southampton with mother, Cassandra, and family friend Martha Lloyd
1809	Attempts, unsuccessfully, to have Crosby publish 'Susan'; moves to Chawton, Hants.
1810	*Sense and Sensibility* accepted by publisher Thomas Egerton
1811	In London, which she visits periodically until 1815, to correct proofs; *Sense and Sensibility* published on commission; starts work on *Mansfield Park*; revises 'First Impressions' as *Pride and Prejudice*
1812	Sells *Pride and Prejudice* to Egerton for £110
1813	*Pride and Prejudice* published; finishes *Mansfield Park*, which Egerton accepts
1814	Begins *Emma*; *Mansfield Park* published on commission
1815	Completes *Emma*; begins *Persuasion*; *Emma* published by John Murray (December, with 1816 on title-page)
1816	Buys back 'Susan' from Crosby and revises as 'Catherine'; completes *Persuasion*; health declining; circumstances reduced on failure of brother Henry's bank
1817	Works on 'Sanditon'; moves with Cassandra to Winchester, where she dies on 18 July; *Northanger Abbey* and *Persuasion* posthumously published by Murray (December, with 1818 on title-page)

REFERENCES

INTRODUCTION

'scribblo-mania': *OED Online*, quoting a Coleridge letter of 1792; 'visitors hold their breath': <https://www.jane-austens-house-museum.org.uk/1-jane-austens-writing-table>; 'casual interruptions': J. E. Austen-Leigh et al., *A Memoir of Jane Austen and Other Family Recollections*, ed. K. Sutherland (2002), 81; 'saying nothing': D. Le Faye, *Jane Austen: A Family Record*, 2nd edn (2003), 206; 'with a pencil': Austen-Leigh et al., *Memoir*, 138; 'misery and oppression': M. Wollstonecraft, *The Wrongs of Woman* (1798), Author's Preface; 'stimulates us to supply': V. Woolf, *The Common Reader*, Series 1 (1925), 139.

CHAPTER 1. JANE AUSTEN PRACTISING

'obliterate a sarcasm': V. Woolf, 'Jane Austen Practising', *New Statesman* (15 July 1922); D. W. Harding, 'Regulated Hatred', *Scrutiny* 8 (1940), 346–62; 'never heard': Austen-Leigh et al., *Memoir*, 140; 'juvenile effusions': Austen-Leigh et al., *Memoir*, 40; 'early scraps': R. W. Chapman (ed.),

Volume the First (1933), ix; 'great amusement', 'early workings', 'nonsensical': Austen-Leigh et al., *Memoir*, 42, 186, 40; 'great burlesques': G. K. Chesterton (ed.), *Love & Freindship* (1922), xi; 'not the appropriate home': M. A. Doody, 'The Early Short Fiction', in E. Copeland and J. McMaster (eds), *The Cambridge Companion to Jane Austen*, 2nd edn (2011), 83–6; 'all that restraint': J. McMaster, *Jane Austen, Young Author* (2016), 70; 'frequently interesting': *Critical Review* (March 1784); 'Plan of a Novel': Jane Austen, *Later Manuscripts*, ed. J. Todd and L. Bree (2008), 228–9; 'Cervantic humour': A. B. Howes, *Laurence Sterne: The Critical Heritage* (1971), 40; 'nonsense tradition': A. Burgess, 'Nonsense', in W. Tigges (ed.), *Explorations in the Field of Nonsense* (1987), 21.

CHAPTER 2. THE TERRORS
OF *NORTHANGER ABBEY*

'calm lives': W. S. Churchill, *The Second World War: Closing the Ring* (1951), 425; 'noise of the populace': D. Le Faye, *Jane Austen's Outlandish Cousin* (2002), 113; 'system of TERROR': C. Emsley, 'An Aspect of Pitt's "Terror"', *Social History* 6.2 (1981), 155; 'marriage had bastilled me': M. Wollstonecraft, *The Wrongs of Woman* (1798), ch. x; W. Godwin, *Caleb Williams*, 2nd edn (1796), Preface; 'Terrorist Novel Writing': E. Clery and R. Miles (eds), *Gothic Documents: A Sourcebook 1700–1820* (2000), 184; 'necessary offspring': Marquis de Sade, *The Crimes of Love*, trans. D. Coward (2005), 13; 'declined by Return': J. Fergus, *Jane Austen: A Literary Life* (1991), 13; 'drafting, redrafting': K. Sutherland,

'Chronology of Composition and Publication', in J. Todd (ed.), *Jane Austen in Context* (2005), 13; R. M. Roche, *The Children of the Abbey* (1796), 1.287–8; R. Warner, *Netley Abbey* (1795), 1.145; 'two kinds of parodies': *The Three Trials of William Hone* (1818), First Trial, 18.

CHAPTER 3. SENSE, SENSIBILITY, SOCIETY

'gruelling criticism': R. West (intr.), *Northanger Abbey* (1932), in B. C. Southam (ed.), *Jane Austen: The Critical Heritage* (1968–87), 2.295; 'character *types*': D. Lynch, *The Economy of Character* (1998), 211; 'morality', 'internal sense': D. Hume, *Moral Philosophy*, ed. G. Sayre-McCord (2006), 78, 187–8; 'weak elegancy', 'gust of feeling': M. Wollstonecraft, *Vindication*, 73, 130; 'intoxicated sensibility', 'born to feel': M. Wollstonecraft, *The Wrongs of Woman* (1798), chs 2, 4; 'look of intelligence': E. I. Spence, *Helen Sinclair* (1799), 2.117; 'wanting sensibility': W. Cowper, *The Task* (1785), 6.560–3; E. S. Barrett, *The Heroine*, 2nd edn (1814), 3.253; 'rival value-systems': M. Butler, *Jane Austen and the War of Ideas*, new edn (1987), 184; 'victory of sense': E. Gunning, *The Orphans of Snowdon* (1797), 2.49; 'mild virtues', 'sense would direct': I. Kelly, *The Abbey of St Asaph* (1795), 1.3; 3.65; 'economic basis': W. H. Auden, 'Letter to Lord Byron' (1937), in Southam (ed.), *Critical Heritage*, 2.299; 'Dostoevsky': W. Empson, '*Sense and Sensibility*' (1936), in Southam (ed.), *Critical Heritage*, 2.298.

CHAPTER 4. THE VOICES
OF *PRIDE AND PREJUDICE*

'dialogue lights up': E. M. Forster reviewing Chapman's edition of Austen, *Nation and Athenaeum* (5 January 1924), in Southam (ed.), *Critical Heritage*, 2.280; 'writing to the moment', 'from the heart': S. Richardson, *Selected Letters*, ed. J. Carroll (1964), 28, 31; 'letter's formal properties': J. Altman, *Epistolarity* (1982), 4; '*first* written in letters': Austen-Leigh et al., *Memoir*, 185; 'full comprehension': W. Scott, *Redgauntlet* (1824), ch. i; 'poor Fanny': H. Fielding, *Joseph Andrews* (1742), I.xi; 'rare lapses', 'ascribe a sex': R. Pascal, *The Dual Voice* (1977), 45; '"it"': M. Bal, *Narratology*, 3rd edn (2009), 15; 'much too clever': Austen-Leigh et al., *Memoir*, 149.

CHAPTER 5. THE SILENCE AT MANSFIELD PARK

'comedy of manners', 'theme after theme', 'cheap slave labor': V. Nabokov, *Lectures on Literature*, ed. F. Bowers (1980), 9, 22, 18; 'ideological and moral affirmations': E. W. Said, *Culture and Imperialism* (1993), 84; 'your bankers sisters Novels': K. Sutherland, 'Jane Austen's Dealings with John Murray and His Firm', *RES* 64 (2012), 108; 'Profits of my Novels': New York Morgan Library, MS. MA 1034.5; 'a heroine': Austen-Leigh et al., *Memoir*, 119; 'menaced with destruction': C. W. Pasley, *Essay on the Military Policy and Institutions of the British Empire* (1810), 1; 'half of the human species': M. Wollstonecraft, *A Vindication of the Rights of Woman*, ed. J. Todd (2008), 225; 'harshness and despotism', 'inalienable rights': P. Knox-Shaw, *Jane Austen and the Enlightenment* (2004), 164, quoting Frank Austen's manuscript 'Remarks on the Island of St Helena' (1808), Royal Naval College, Greenwich.

CHAPTER 6. *EMMA* AND ENGLISHNESS

'dear Jane': H. James, 'The Lesson of Balzac' (1905), in Southam (ed.), *Critical Heritage*, 2.230; 'delineates with great accuracy': *Gentleman's Magazine* (September 1816), in Southam (ed.), *Critical Heritage*, 1.79; 'laid in higher life', W. Scott reviewing *Emma*, *Quarterly Review* (March 1816), in Southam (ed.), *Critical Heritage*, 1.68; 'Bow-Wow Strain': W. Scott, journal entry for 14 March 1826, in Southam (ed.), *Critical Heritage*, 1.113; 'A Revolution': *The Letters of William and Dorothy Wordsworth, Vol. 3, Pt 2: 1812–1820*, ed. E. De Selincourt, M. Moorman, and A. G. Hill (1969), 375; Sir Simon Steeltrap: T. L. Peacock, *Crotchet Castle*, ed. F. Johnston and M. Bevis (2016), 49.

CHAPTER 7. PASSION AND *PERSUASION*

'delineating the surface': C. Brontë, letter to W. S. Williams (12 April 1850), in Southam (ed.), *Critical Heritage*, 1.140–1; 'pinched and narrow': R. W. Emerson, journal entry of 5 August 1861, in Southam (ed.), *Critical Heritage*, 1.25; 'dull, stupid': E. Pound, reviewing Robert Frost's *North of Boston*, *Poetry* (December 1914), in Southam (ed.), *Critical Heritage*, 2.84; 'concentrated feeling': H. James, letter to G. Pellew (23 June 1883), 2.180; 'typical "Austen novel"': D. S. Lynch (intr.), *Persuasion* (2004), x–xi; 'Jane Austen had loved': V. Woolf, 'Jane Austen at Sixty' (1923), in Southam (ed.), *Critical Heritage*, 2.282; 'description of the place': H. Tennyson, *Alfred Lord Tennyson: A Memoir by His Son* (1897), 2.47; 'dying dinosaurs': P. W. Graham, *Jane Austen and Charles Darwin: Naturalists and Novelists* (2008), 179.

AFTERWORD

'already perceptible': V. Woolf, 'Jane Austen at Sixty' (1923), in Southam (ed.), *Critical Heritage*, 2.283.

FURTHER READING

BIOGRAPHY AND REFERENCE

Paula Byrne, *The Real Jane Austen: A Life in Small Things* (HarperCollins, 2013).

Edward Copeland and Juliet McMaster (eds), *The Cambridge Companion to Jane Austen*, 2nd edn (Cambridge University Press, 2011).

J. A. Downie (ed.), *The Oxford Handbook of the Eighteenth-Century Novel* (Oxford University Press, 2016).

Jan Fergus, *Jane Austen: A Literary Life* (Macmillan, 1991).

Peter Garside, James Raven, Rainer Schöwerling, et al., *The English Novel 1770–1829: A Bibliographical Survey* (Oxford University Press, 2000).

Peter Garside and Karen O'Brien (eds), *The Oxford History of the Novel in English, Volume 2: English and British Fiction 1750–1820* (Oxford University Press, 2015).

David Gilson, *A Bibliography of Jane Austen*, 2nd edn (St Paul's Bibliographies, 1997).

Park Honan, *Jane Austen: Her Life* (Weidenfeld and Nicolson, 1987).

Claudia L. Johnson and Clara Tuite (eds), *A Companion to Jane Austen* (Wiley-Blackwell, 2009).

Deirdre Le Faye, *A Chronology of Jane Austen and her Family 1600–2000*, 2nd edn (Cambridge University Press, 2013).

Deirdre Le Faye, *Jane Austen: A Family Record*, 2nd edn (Cambridge University Press, 2003).

Devoney Looser, *The Cambridge Companion to Women's Writing in the Romantic Period* (Cambridge University Press, 2015).

Lawrence W. Mazzeno, *Jane Austen: Two Centuries of Criticism* (Camden House, 2011).

David Nokes, *Jane Austen: A Life* (Fourth Estate, 1997).

William St Clair, *The Reading Nation in the Romantic Period* (Cambridge University Press, 2004).

B. C. Southam, *Jane Austen: The Critical Heritage*, 2 vols (Routledge, 1968–87).

Fiona Stafford, *Jane Austen: A Brief Life* (Yale University Press, 2017).

Janet Todd (ed.), *Jane Austen in Context* (Cambridge University Press, 2005).

Lucy Worsley, *Jane Austen at Home* (Hodder & Stoughton, 2017).

CRITICISM

Janine Barchas, *Matters of Fact in Jane Austen: History, Location, and Celebrity* (Johns Hopkins University Press, 2012).

Joe Bray, *The Language of Jane Austen* (Palgrave Macmillan, 2018).

Marilyn Butler, *Jane Austen and the War of Ideas*, new edn (Clarendon Press, 1987).

Jenny Davidson, *Reading Jane Austen* (Cambridge University Press, 2017).

Margaret Doody, *Jane Austen's Names: Riddles, Persons, Places* (University of Chicago Press, 2015).

Alistair M. Duckworth, *The Improvement of the Estate: A Study of Jane Austen's Novels* (Johns Hopkins Press, 1971).

William H. Galperin, *The Historical Austen* (University of Pennsylvania Press, 2003).

Katie Halsey, *Jane Austen and Her Readers, 1786–1945* (Anthem, 2012).

Jocelyn Harris, *Jane Austen's Art of Memory* (Cambridge University Press, 1989).

Jill Heydt-Stevenson, *Austen's Unbecoming Conjunctions: Subversive Laughter, Embodied History* (Palgrave Macmillan, 2005).

Richard Jenkyns, *A Fine Brush on Ivory: An Appreciation of Jane Austen* (Oxford University Press, 2004).

Claudia L. Johnson, *Jane Austen: Women, Politics, and the Novel* (University of Chicago Press, 1988).

Peter Knox-Shaw, *Jane Austen and the Enlightenment* (Cambridge University Press, 2004).

Devoney Looser, *The Making of Jane Austen* (Johns Hopkins University Press, 2017).

Deidre Shauna Lynch (ed.), *Janeites: Austen's Disciples and Devotees* (Princeton University Press, 2000).

Juliet McMaster, *Jane Austen, Young Author* (Ashgate, 2016).

Anthony Mandal, *Jane Austen and the Popular Novel: The Determined Author* (Palgrave Macmillan, 2007).

D. A. Miller, *Jane Austen, or The Secret of Style* (Princeton University Press, 2003).

John Mullan, *What Matters in Jane Austen?* (Bloomsbury, 2013).

Kathryn Sutherland, *Jane Austen's Textual Lives: From Aeschylus to Bollywood* (Oxford University Press, 2005).

Bharat Tandon, *Jane Austen and the Morality of Conversation* (Anthem, 2003).

Tony Tanner, *Jane Austen* (Macmillan, 1986).

Janet Todd, *The Cambridge Introduction to Jane Austen*, 2nd edn (Cambridge University Press, 2015).

Clara Tuite, *Romantic Austen: Sexual Politics and the Literary Canon* (Cambridge University Press, 2002).

Karen Valihora, *Austen's Oughts: Judgment after Locke and Shaftesbury* (University of Delaware Press, 2010).

Mary Waldron, *Jane Austen and the Fiction of Her Time* (Cambridge University Press, 1999).

John Wiltshire, *The Hidden Jane Austen* (Cambridge University Press, 2014).

INDEX

For technical reasons connected with digital access, index entries point to the full paragraph in which an indexed term occurs. On occasion, terms indicated by a two-page span (e.g. 4–5) may appear on only one of those pages. For the same reasons, a longer span (e.g. 90–3) does not necessarily indicate continuous discussion.

Index